LIGHTING FIRES

Deepening education through meditation

JÖRGEN SMIT

Translated by Simon Blaxland-de-Lange

HAWTHORN PRESS

Originally published in German by
Verlag Freies Geistesleben as *Der Werdende Mensch*

English translation *Lighting Fires*
Copyright © 1992 Hawthorn Press

Published by Hawthorn Press,
Hawthorn House, 1 Lansdown Lane, Lansdown,
Stroud, Gloucestershire, GL5 1BJ, UK
Tel: (01453) 757040 Fax: (01453) 751138
www.hawthornpress.com

Typeset by Glevum Graphics, Gloucestershire

First edition, 1992
Reprinted in 2001 by The Bath Press, Bath

ISBN 1 869 890 45 0

CONTENTS

PREFACE

The essays gathered together in this book are based on lectures which Jörgen Smit, the then Leader of the Pedagogical Section of the School of Spiritual Science at the Goetheanum, gave between 1984 and 1988 either in public (in the case of the first) or before Waldorf teachers. They have been published in the journal *Erziehungskunst* (Essay 1) and in the internal teachers' circular of the Waldorf Schools (Essays 2–4).

The publisher has decided to make them accessible to a wider public by means of the present volume, as the hints which they contain on how education can be made more fruitful through the meditative path of knowledge of Anthroposophy are of value for anyone who works and lives with children or adolescents. As the original lectures were, in part, presented to listeners familiar with Anthroposophy, the basic elements of Anthroposophy are presupposed, so that concepts such as 'etheric body' or 'astral body' are not given any further explanation. The reader who is not familiar with them may wish to consult the basic books of Rudolf Steiner, such as *Theosophy* and *Occult Science – An Outline*, published by Rudolf Steiner Press, Forest Row, East Sussex, RH18 5JB, United Kingdom.

Jörgen Smit's intention in these essays is to address 'man in the becoming', the emerging human being who lives not only in each child but also in every adult. Education is in this sense always also a part of self-education.

ONE

The teacher's path of schooling

The expression 'the teacher's path of schooling' brings into a single focus two avenues of development. On the one hand there is the exact knowledge of the particular subject that the teacher wishes to convey to the pupils: The mathematics teacher must, for example, master his material; he must be well practised in mathematical thinking and constantly developing it further. And on the other hand, there is a need for the teacher to have a pedagogical method whereby he is able to impart something to his pupils. Thus, in addition to having a good knowledge of his subject, he must also have mastered and cultivated the means of imparting what he knows.

It would be very easy but questionable if one were to assign a view of the world and of man such as Anthroposophy — which reaches out far beyond the areas to which we have referred — a significance for educational practice. A glance at the principal streams of educational theory may serve to illustrate this.

Two streams in particular can clearly be distinguished. On the one hand there are those educationalists who strongly maintain that what matters is not so much specific knowledge or a particular pedagogical technique but, rather, the whole

attitude to life and world outlook of the teachers and how this
enters into education. This holds good for those educationalists who are firmly wedded to a particular religious creed and
also for those who reject all religious creeds as mere super-
stition in favour of ethical principles of a more abstract kind.
These religious creeds or the corresponding non-religious
ethical creeds are then regarded as the 'main thing' which
should give the whole educational process its backbone. On
the other hand there are those educationalists who affirm the
exact opposite, that the attitude to life and the world outlook
of the teacher should not play any part in the practice of
education, that this belongs, as it were, to a different department. Examples are then cited — by educationalists of this
latter kind, for instance — as a way of verifying these assertions.

There is the case of a thoroughly capable teacher with a real
gift, who has by no means had a lot of training or experience.
When such a 'born teacher' enters the classroom for the first
time, he immediately has a connection with the children.
One can really see how the children want to learn something
from him, how there is a give and take between him and the
children. But if one were to ask such a teacher about his
world outlook or his image of man, it might be perfectly
possible that this outstanding teacher would talk a load of
nonsense about these matters, because he has not developed
in this direction. Nevertheless, he is an excellent teacher!
Thus it can be shown that world outlooks and knowledge of
men do not have much to do with the practice of education.

Another example. A teacher who has studied a great deal,
is thoroughly familiar with all manner of educational sys-
tems, has a brilliant university degree and so forth, enters a
school classroom — and everything goes wrong. The children have not the slightest interest in what he is saying. His

wealth of knowledge is of no use to him at all. He is complete-ly incapable of establishing a relationship to the children.

These are two examples which serve as a foundation for the views of many educationalists, those who say that world outlook and knowledge of man are separate from what is enacted 'in another department' as the actual practising of education.

Others may perhaps add ironically: 'World outlooks and knowledge of man have their place in official speeches or in the leading articles of educational journals. There one should say something about Pestalozzi or about human dignity, and then one gets down to business, to the actual job in hand.'

Anyone who takes issue with these assertions has to admit that they contain a lot of truth; and they should not be lightly disregarded. However, the following can be set over and against this attitude. In recent years there have been a whole series of investigations (published in Scandinavian journals), where in connection with questionnaires and interviews with several thousand young people it was asked: 'How do you think about the future? What hopes do you have for your later life? How do you imagine life after the year 2000?' What was remarkable was that seventy-five per cent of these young people looked without hope towards the future and said something to this effect: 'I do not believe in a future, it is a black hole into which I am looking, I believe that everything is going to rack and ruin and that life will no longer be possible in the next millennium'. Seventy-five per cent of the young people who were asked were of such an opinion.

Now there are, of course, always young people whose views of the future are somewhat coloured by melancholia or hypochondria, so that any survey would have to reckon with some ten per cent of such answers. But seventy-five per cent? That has probably never happened before, for after all it lies in the nature of youth to be hopeful and positive. As a young person one has a capacity for enthusiasm! To be sure, many hopes fade or show themselves to be deceptions, but then new hopes arise. A healthy young person enters into life with strength and enthusiasm. But now there are among these young people seventy-five per cent who look without hope upon the future as a 'black hole'! And there is no knowledge, no pedagogical technique of the teacher which can be of any avail, however much it may have been deepened by individual capacities. The problem lies far, far deeper. It has to do with man's inmost core. A young person without a future is crippled in his or her whole attitude to life. This has significant consequences, as much for thinking and feeling as it has for the life of will.

All human evolution bears, more or less unconsciously, a hopeful, forward-looking attitude, a loving devotion for learning to work and working to learn, where man reaches out beyond himself, beyond his present situation. The future is then of course — in spite of difficulties, in spite of all the hindrances and set-backs which may emerge — bright and full of promise and stirs the will into enthusiastic involvement. But if the future is regarded as essentially black and hopeless, the inner power of development *must* be blunted thereby.

What happens with one's thinking when it encounters this paralyzing influence? It becomes in all instances superficial, for one is considering the facts purely externally if one says that everything is going to rack and ruin. One is not really interested in the matter at hand. In feeling, where one is always connected with the world and flows together with it, a person for whom the world looks black is only relating to himself. Then feeling becomes sick, it becomes entangled in itself. And willing? Either it becomes completely paralyzed, so that one no longer has any initiative, or — in the case of someone with a choleric tendency — the will is raised to brutality. Unbridled, brutal acts of violence will then ensue.

The problems that now appear have to do with man's innermost powers of development, and we must ask ourselves. 'Can teachers, parents or educators offer any help from deeper sources to children or adolescents? Can they arouse in the young people — amidst all else — something that may be learnt?'

Such a realm would indeed have priority over all the other knowledge and abilities that the teacher must cultivate within himself. For if the educator is able to address man's innermost powers of development, there are in all cases hopes for the future for the children.

———————

Let us consider the being of man. In orthodox educational science there are two large realms which are more or less strongly emphasized in their significance for education. These are, on the one hand, genetics and, on the other, sociology.

The science of genetics inclines to the view that everything is already predetermined by the genes, by the purely physical, and that all that needs to be done is to unfold what is there. Sociologists on the other hand, do acknowledge the need to be aware of the genetic foundation but lay far more emphasis upon influences from the environment. What a person *is* depends entirely upon the influences from his surroundings, his parents, society, and so on. If one applies this view to, for example, Mozart, this leads to the extreme position of saying that everyone could be a Mozart if he were to grow up under the same conditions as Mozart did.

In this manner of thinking there is something that is not taken into account, and that lies in the existential question which as an adult human being one can always ask oneself: 'What are you doing now in this moment out of your life situation?' A certain individual is in a particular life situation, in which there are, shall we say, an especially large number of difficulties. He does, of course, bear certain predispositions within himself, and there are also determining factors from without. But if one were simply to add together what works from within and what influences the person from without and were to let an action issue from the result, one would have completely lost sight of the reality. For in an actual situation there always arises the question as to how I can take the substance of my life *into my own hands*, so as to develop to a new stage beyond myself.

It is always possible that I do nothing, in which case I remain as I am and become approximately a product of what issues from the body and of what works in a determining way out of the surrounding world. Then I begin to become approximately — though not entirely — like a thing. I lose my own humanity.

Let us try to clarify these two aspects by means of the example of a little child. Most little children have a 'crawling phase' before they are able to stand upright. There are exceptions, where the little child goes directly from sitting to adopting a vertical posture, but that is rare. Most children have a 'crawling phase' of varying duration when they slide around on the floor, and at which they develop considerable proficiency, before they manifest any desire to stand upright. One might almost believe that they were going to stay there for ever. And then this uprightness comes, though two preconditions are necessary. In the first place, the human form must be fashioned in such a way that uprightness is possible. In the case of a person who is crippled, he would not be able to stand upright however much effort he might make. Thus there is a precondition from the physical side. There must be a human form that is sufficiently healthy. This creates the *possibility* for uprightness, though it does not necessarily result. The child could carry on crawling if the power of uprightness was not kindled within the context of this possibility.

The child is surrounded by adults who move in an upright position, and there is in the child a strong power of imitation through which everything is perceived. Thus the child perceives these upright forms — but does it *have* to imitate them? Certain preconditions with regard to the surroundings and the body must be fulfilled, but then comes what is even so quite astonishing: the child does *indeed* stand upright and takes its first steps. It has reached a new stage as regards what it has been hitherto. In both these respects a mighty power of development is manifested in the child which now forms a foundation for the whole of the rest of its life.

There are naturally many who will be unable to recall this point in their own biography, although there are those who return wholly to this time, the first moment of uprightness, to this *exultant* joy. But even if one does not have this, one can study small children and feel and experience what is going on in this moment.

This process can be compared with another process, namely with what happens if we do not allow the child to enter into uprightness on its own but give it a walking-machine with the help of which it is meant to stand. Unfortunately, it frequently happens — not very often but nevertheless too often —

that impatient parents are unable to wait for the right moment of maturity. Then they give the child an apparatus with a frame on wheels and with straps attached to it. The child, unable to attain an upright posture on its own, is strapped into this frame and moves its feet, although it can neither stand nor walk. It trundles about with this apparatus looking as though it is walking. What is going on here? It is a forestalling of development — immaturity! This can be used as a picture for profound laws that hold good in later life, both with children and also with adolescents and adults.

A certain stage must first be lived through before one has the maturity and the capacity to ascend to a new stage. Only then can one enter into the new stage in a wholly inward way and develop further to the next stage. Here we are confronted with man's *maturing capacity of becoming* on the steps of his path of development.

Piaget, the famous Swiss educationalist and psychologist, has in association with his research collected extensive material with which he has been able to observe a number of stages with respect to various faculties in the development of the child. The results of this research have opened the eyes of many educators, because they have realized that they had, for example, been speaking with nine-year-old children as if they were twelve.[1] They had completely disregarded the developmental stages of children with respect to, for example, the relationship between thinking and language, and had failed to see that in the eleventh year the child crosses a certain threshold where the relationship of its thinking to language changes. Until the eleventh year thinking is carried so strongly by language and bound up with it that work, sense-perception, mental picture and concept form a living whole and cannot be separated from one another in the same clear sense as with adults. The conscious distinction between the word and the abstract concept belonging to it only develops clearly after the eleventh year.

Of course, there are always exceptions to these laws of development, i.e. a variation over a shorter or longer period (1 – 2 years). Through Piaget's research, these teachers were now able to take such developmental stages of children into consideration.

Other educationalists have, however, been unimpressed by this. Piaget may indeed have proved the existence of certain thresholds of development, but what is to prevent teachers from lowering these thresholds? Children can, after all, be trained! I believe that these teachers are perfectly right. It is possible to lower these thresholds in child development, but then something happens very similar to what is going on with the walking-machine: a step forward in development is taken artificially and this has a disastrous effect upon man's being — a lack of maturity!

To know or to be able to do something does not mean that one has developed the maturity for it. If the necessary maturity is lacking, this leads to a superficial knowledge which one may perhaps be able to reproduce in an examination but which one has not really made one's own. The appropriate level of maturity is not of course laid down, since every individual develops differently and has his own standard of maturity. But in the maturity there are essential qualities which are of significance in each case.

With every sense-impression we open ourselves up towards the world. In all sense-impressions there is something of the element of *love*. When we perceive a blue sky or a green meadow, we as it were reach lovingly into them. But then it becomes a little too much for us, and we thrust the impression away to some extent. When a person speaks, we listen lovingly to what he has to say. But suddenly it becomes too much, and we withdraw, we seek to keep the impression at a distance and adopt an attitude of *antipathy*.

In all our relationships to the world we have these two qualities, that we first open ourselves to and unite ourselves with the world and then assert ourselves. Both belong together. Between these two polarities a delicate interweaving arises, out of which alone development can go forward.

These two tendencies are also to be found in the soul-world. I should like — using a somewhat peculiar image — to refer to them as the 'rubber attitude' and the 'plasticine attitude'. If one takes a rubber ball and presses it, the impression vanishes without leaving any trace. Similarly, there is a tendency in man to assert himself to the same degree that something works upon him from without.

But if one takes a piece of plasticine and presses into it, the impression remains. Thus there is also another tendency in man, that of allowing oneself to be strongly impressed upon by the outer world. Of course, one will not find anyone who has only the one or the other tendency. But there are those who have much of the 'rubber attitude' — robust, assertive people whom one can address without this making any impression upon them at all. They stay as they are, however old they may be. Then there are others who bear to a considerable degree the impressions of what their father, mother and teacher have told them. Even if a new experience comes their way, it lies above what went before as a different layer. Thus, these people are continually having new impressions which are all retained.

Naturally, everyone must have something of both, otherwise he would not be a human being. For as long as he only adopts the 'plasticine attitude' the person concerned will not arrive at individual development. He remains a product of the outer world. While for as long as he only asserts himself in the 'rubber attitude', no development takes place, for he simply stays the way he is.[2]

A meaningful development on the part of man can take place only if both qualities are united. One begins with the one aspect, where something is taken in from without; certain inner powers have already been developed, but one is interested in what is happening outside of one and so holds oneself back. One adopts to some extent a 'plasticine attitude'. However, one does not stop there but inwardly intensifies the impression with a strong activity of one's own, so that a threefold step comes about. First, a strong inner development must take place, then one has to draw back and open oneself up in an act of surrender to the world. One does not, however, remain with this gesture of openness but begins to intensify what has been newly acquired. With this a new stage is reached, and this fact can be perceived in all development as a power in the person concerned.

Just as the little child enters into uprightness and so reaches a new stage, so can the adult also acquire a sense of uprightness by examining himself, as it were from above, and saying to himself: 'You have been living in a certain way, but things cannot carry on as before.' He wakes up and leaves the stage where he has been. However, this can happen only through the threefold step referred to above, where one opens oneself up to something new and then elaborates upon what one has received. The stronger this developmental power is in the person concerned, the more impossible it becomes to look upon a future that is black. One has perceived mankind's infinite powers of development, and, however dark everything may appear to be around one, it is always possible to say to oneself: 'That is only what is given, the material: the question is what shall I do with it?' Now one has a strong conviction of this power of development, because one feels it within oneself, and knows that it is present and exerts an influence. There are all manner of stages at which the individual can perceive this power of development within himself. It may be no more than an intuitive feeling, which nevertheless clearly says: 'You can develop further, you are not finished, you are not condemned to be overwhelmed from without by all kinds of influences; you can constantly awaken new forces from within for the accomplishing of your tasks.'

Little by little this can be grasped more consciously. The individual learns to know the springs of his eternal being, for which every earthly life-situation is only the material — an exercise, an opportunity — whereby the imperfect human being develops towards true manhood.

And the converse? The less this power of development is active, the more dependent one is upon a hopeless outward situation. Then the dismal outlook of the present — the pollution of the environment, the famine and wars all over the world — will become altogether overpowering. One enters oneself into a state of hopelessness. In this way the power of development in the individual and in human communities is overwhelmed. Herein lies one of the most terrible soul-sicknesses of the present. With this we return to the question we posed at the beginning as to what a teacher in a school can do when confronted with this ever more widespread sense of hopelessness?

Of course, the teacher must have a thorough knowledge of his subject, and, equally, he must know how to impart it to the children. Both qualities must, however, enter deeply into the developing aspect of man's being. Only in such a way can the teacher support the children in their development. He cannot simply thrust something at them, for then he would be treating them like plasticine. But he can encourage them in such a way that the interest is stirred within them to work independently with what has been given. Only then does real maturity arise in accordance with the appropriate level for the age. This power of maturity also helps to make it possible for grief and opposition to be borne, and gives a certain inner mood of happiness. Only when children and adolescents are able to make this power active within themselves will the teacher help them further on their way.

In this area lies the central significance of the anthroposoph-ical path of training, for the forces which are unconsciously active in the child when it learns to walk, to speak and to think, and also in later childhood, are the same as those which the adult stirs into activity when he consciously prog-resses to higher stages of his development and knowledge. The child and the adolescent know nothing of the workings of these powers of development, while the adult can take hold of them consciously and work independently towards culti-vating them.

The awakening of the powers of development inherent in man is, of course, possible in all life-situations and in every calling. What is special about being a teacher is that this universally human aspect is directed towards educational work itself. Let us consider this anthroposophical path of training!

The first form of exercise is the intensification of the inner powers of imagination. By this is meant the following: in ordinary life, in a town for example, thousands of impres-sions thrust themselves upon us from the 'outer world' through advertising, television and newspapers. Now the corresponding inner power must be developed whereby all

sense-impressions are shut out: we need to cultivate the
conscious building-up of an inner picture, so that we paint it
inwardly with forms and colours so strongly and clearly that
it makes more impression on us than anything that we behold
outwardly. For example, we may be studying with open eyes
a rose with green leaves and red blossom. Now we shut our
eyes and try inwardly to paint the image of the rose. Then we
compare these two impressions in their strength, the warmth
of the red and the luscious green that we behold with our eyes
open compared with what arises within us when we have
painted a rose with our eyes shut.

Many people of the present time are not, however, able
inwardly to build up a coloured image of the rose. They can
only experience it as grey, since they are to so great a degree
dependent upon outward impressions that their inner powers
of imagination are paralyzed. To be sure, that does not mean
that this power cannot unfold, for it can be trained. Thus one
contemplates the redness of the rose, shuts one's eyes and
begins to *feel* this red. It will at first continue to be grey if one
seeks to paint it inwardly. If so, one studies the perception
repeatedly; for what is of principal significance is that if one
does not feel anything through one's sense-impressions, if
one experiences the qualities of red, green, blue, etc., in a
merely indifferent way, one engenders in oneself a grey mood
of soul. But if one enters with one's feelings into every
sense-impression in a deep and differentiated way (for each
impression has its own specific echo), one can give rise to an
inner imagination that is richly imbued with feelings.[3] This is
an indication of a first step on the path of training of a strong
inner life. But what does it signify for the teacher?

When children from the first to the twelfth class have the
teacher in any particular realm of study before them, the
teacher represents the whole world and the child yearns to

receive this. But if the teacher forms his lessons in such a way that they are superficial or merely convey information, this offers scanty nourishment for the children. When the child is seven years of age, a tender potential for an inner imaginative faculty awakens in its soul, both in the form of memories and of imaginations; and this faculty is different from before the seventh year. Before this time too, the child has memory, recollection and imagination, but as yet these are still present in the sense-experiences of the body.

After the seventh year of life these powers are emancipated, and a new law makes its presence felt. The child can now, quite irrespective of outer sense-impressions, give birth to something within itself, and it can learn much in this inner world. This begins in a very small and tender way in the first class, and so this is the point where the teacher can begin his lessons. To this end, he must work beforehand with every subject of the lesson in such a way that he carries in himself an inner picture of it. Then he will be able to speak in a different way to the children and a clear sense of life arises in the classroom, so that one can observe how the children listen in a different way. But if the teacher has merely read something in a book and has perhaps learnt it by heart without having an inner picture of it, then however much he may tell the children he will be at cross-purposes with them. They will be stirred by something, an outward fascination arises, remains for a moment, and then goes away again. But if the educator has worked with every aspect of what he relates by means of this inner living picture, one may then see how the children begin to *breathe* differently. They are living with the substance of the lesson, and one can really see how these pictures are beginning to grow within them.

However, this only represents the first step, for the teacher might now fall into a terrible temptation. If he discovers what an effect his words have upon the children, this can be immensely fascinating and highly dangerous. He sees the whole class in front of him and how they take in the wonderful pictures, and as he tells them more and more he begins *to enjoy himself*. Thus, all this is only a first stage, where the teacher gives 'nourishment' to the children. Now the next stage must follow, where he must withdraw in favour of the children. Initially he has something and is able to give something to the children — self-assertion. Then follows the second stage, where he draws back. But this, too, is not a place to linger, for then comes the third stage — working out of one's own forces. The children now need to begin something with what has been given. This can perhaps only happen the following day through memory exercises, artistic exercises and so on. The children must in every aspect of their work be able to do something in order to take it further, otherwise they become falsely dependent and inwardly slack. How does the teacher reach this stage? It is not easy for him, for he must now to a certain extent 'creep into' the children. By this is meant not a mystical experience but something absolutely concrete.

But how does one get to know the children? One must first observe precisely how they behave, how they look, how they move, speak and so on. Exact psychological observation is therefore the first requirement. The second step is sympathy in the sense that one enters with one's feelings into what is going on in the moment. This is, however, only one aspect. The other aspect is only too easily neglected in favour of the first, which in the case of the majority of capable teachers is well developed. The teacher must ask himself: 'How was I myself when I was the same age as these children? Is it possible for me to return to the stage when I was seven years old, so that I may discover inwardly the essential nature of this age?'

For this an additional long path of training is needed. Now it is not the inwardly intensified power of imagination that is being schooled but one has rather to work slowly and thoroughly upon one's own life. Supposing that a teacher is twenty-five years old and is now looking back to the time when he was eighteen years old. How is he to do this? First he must summon up his memories and experience once again what happened at that time. This alone is not enough, for now he must try to look upon this situation *from above* as though he were someone else. He must separate himself from himself and consider what is essential and what is inessential. We have here to do with a fundamental exercise of the anthroposophical path of knowledge. There are many who attempt this exercise but who only manage the first step. They are unable to decide what was essential and what inessential, and do not progress any further.

How does one acquire the capacity to distinguish between the essential and the inessential? There is a key with which one can gain access to this question. Let us take an example. A certain person was in a difficult situation where a friend insulted him, thus wounding him sorely. He can recall that he said to himself something like this: 'That is unjust, what he said to me is not right and I shall not let myself feel offended'. In this way — as we may presuppose for the sake of our example — the insult was *overcome*. What was of principal importance in this event, the substance of the insult or the power wherewith the insult could be overcome? The *substance* of the insult has no importance when compared with the *power* through which the insult was overcome. Therein lies the key! When in the course of an evening-review *(Rückschau)* one seeks to know what is essential, one must focus one's attention upon the powers that were

developed in a particular life-situation. In this way one encounters what is of real importance and which has far greater
significance than the purely superficial happenings of the
moment.

Once this stage is reached, a further question arises;
namely, how it was possible that a certain situation arose in
the first place? Now it is that the *other people involved* come
more strongly to the fore. If one had been alone, the situation
described would not have arisen at all, and no new powers
could have been developed. Thus the others were necessary
and indispensable to this process. In this way one recognizes
the profound significance of other people for one's own
destiny.

At first, everyone has a false, though quite natural, idea as
he reviews his life: he believes himself to be a centre around
whom other people gather. We always see ourselves as the
great focal-point with respect to other people, who appear on
the periphery as mere statistics. Only when the evening-
review is practised do we recognize their significance, and
through this the initially great focus of our own ego becomes
ever smaller until it completely disappears. Then the question is justified: 'Am I only a centre, only in me, am I not
equally in others?' We begin to experience a higher level of
our own self in other people and we feel that we are not
separated from them. This higher element works throughout
the whole of life and it now gradually begins to dawn. That is,
therefore, the second aspect of the path of training, which we
can now summarize: first, the review, remembering what
happened, then objectivising and looking at ourselves from
above; the question of the essential and the non-essential;
becoming attentive to the powers inherent in our own evolution; and finally raising ourselves up to other people, so as
gradually to find the higher unity of our own self.[4]

This must now be accomplished backwards through one's whole life to the stage of one's life equivalent to the children whom one is educating. In this way one approaches the children from within and not from without. The teacher experiences what is essential about a particular stage of life and how the children themselves experience it.

That is the prerequisite for the teacher being able to draw back. He must first have developed strong inner forces so that he has something to give. But then he must draw back and 'creep into' the children. By this means he creates a space in which the children can work independently with the material that the teacher has imparted.

The training path of the adult, its spiritual development with the two pillars of the strengthening of inner forces and the assimilation of one's own life, is well-suited to serve the development of children. The teacher perceives the importance of these two pillars for his work, though they can, of course, be employed in other professions, in a manner appropriate to any particular situation. If he were only to carry out the review of his life, he would indeed have a deep understanding of the children; but he would not be able to bring them anything. On the other hand, if he had only cultivated inner powers of imagination, he would have much to tell the children but without leaving them free. Thus both aspects belong together as a right and a left hand. The more these two powers are strengthened, the less will man gaze hopelessly into a black future.

If a person is in a difficult life-situation with considerable social tensions and in a poor physical state, he can be sure that every difficult, initially overwhelming, situation has at least two quite different causes arising from a failure to master certain things. On the one hand, one is inwardly too weak and sluggish, with insufficient development of spiritual initiative or creative imagination. On the other hand, one has too little insight into one's life-situation, into one's relationship to the world and to other people. Often one will not find a simple and direct way forward. But it is always possible to do something and to avail oneself of both pillars of the path of training: first the strengthening of one's inner spiritual power, without which no further step is possible but with which alone one would become a mere egoist. Then working through one's own life in such a way that one strips oneself down piece by piece, so that one enters ever more and more into others, into the world. A breathing-process begins to take place between the intensifying of one's own activity and entering with one's feelings into others. Thus the whole is heightened ever more and more into a growing power.

But what does this power bear within itself? It bears the future within itself, for the individual can now make for himself a picture of the future (even if the details cannot be seen); it is the formative power of humanity. I can find this power within me, and thereby feel myself to be united with others. Out of this interplay of the two exercises an unshakable hope for the future results. However, this is not the case if one only carries out one of the exercises. It lives in the oscillation between the two, in man's power of uprightness.

Just as one regains one's uprightness in a particular life-situation, so can this power be used as one meets the children. In them there are infinite, hidden and unobserved powers, which can now gradually, little by little — not too quick, or else one resorts to walking-machines — be awoken.

If we place these requirements before us, we may see what is lacking at the present time. There is no lack of specialized knowledge, which is developed to the Nth degree through computers; there is no lack of specific capabilities. What is lacking is a sufficient awareness and an adequate cultivation of these powers of development, which represent a maturing force within man and among humanity.

If we observe politicians and ask ourselves: 'Do they have insufficient intelligence? Is that the cause of all the misunderstandings in the world? Do they lack knowledge?' No, that is not the case, for they have very high IQs and immense knowledge — with certain exceptions. What is lacking, however, is an inner maturity of the powers of development, the feeling for what is essential. These qualities are strongly underdeveloped, especially in the highly civilized industrial countries.

Here lie great tasks for the future. The individual cannot accomplish them on his own, however, for this is possible only through co-operation. In this respect, the Rudolf Steiner schools have a particular task. It is not only the individual teacher who must follow a path of training and development but also the College in the school community. This will not be achieved for a long time, not even in Rudolf Steiner schools. They are often far from being able to do this. Here, too, there lies a training-ground for the future.

I have tried to show that world-conception and knowledge of man should not be understood in a purely superficial sense but should be developed and practised on the path of training. Only then can world-conception and knowledge of man enter in a dynamic way into daily life.

TWO

The awakening of consciousness in the etheric

'The awakening of consciousness in the etheric' is a theme which has a special importance. But first it needs further elucidation. A particular problem, indeed almost a condition of sickness, is the gulf that everyone finds today between his inner experiences and his experiences of a world that is imagined as superficially material. What is experienced in the material-physical world has a nature that is alien to all moral, spiritual qualities. And on the other hand, wherever the spiritual manifests itself it abides in a certain subjective inwardness and does not take hold of the physical-material world. It remains isolated. The endeavours of Anthroposophy towards a path of knowledge which leads to the spiritual in man and from the spiritual in man to the spiritual in the universe[1] (hence to a bridging of this gulf) can only be successful if the spiritual is experienced so strongly and so concretely that it is brought into the physical and into activity in the physical-material realm, if the physical-material realm does not remain unheeded but the spirit is liberated from it. But one can only make the transition from the spiritual realm of being to the physical realm of matter through the realm of the etheric, and similarly one can only reach from the physical world of the senses to a liberation of the spiritual that works within it through this same realm, which borders directly on the physical world of the senses but cannot be apprehended by one's ordinary consciousness. Hence the special significance of the awakening of consciousness in the etheric! If consciousness disappears from this realm, or is subdued, we live in the gulf between the other two realms, in a state of schizophrenia.

All thoughts 'even if they do indeed spring from the spiritual, from the etheric world (and without it the thoughts would not exist at all)' appear in our consciousness only as shadows, as thoughts existing within us. On the other side is the whole realm of sense-perceptions. This world, too, stems from the sources of the spiritual realm of being and thrusts itself on our attention from the other side, but it does not enter as something living into our consciousness but fades into a phantom-like phenomenon where we apprehend individual percepts only by means of mental images of the objects. Thus we do not live in a spiritual reality, neither from the inward side in the spiritual realm of thinking nor from the outward side in the spiritual realm of the sense-world; we live instead in the gulf between the phantoms of sense perceptions and the shadows of thoughts. On both sides darkness as compared with true reality. The wonderful thing is that we can reach true reality, though not without effort. We don't get it 'for nothing'.

We only free ourselves from the realm of shadow and phantoms through our activity in the quest for knowledge. Even though this quest for knowledge is not in itself shadowy, it initially appears to our consciousness as something shadowy or phantom-like. In its foundations there is, however, something deeper which works imperceptibly in living activity. But this alone will not lead to any result unless the cognitive power is inwardly — gradually, through training — strengthened, initially without anything definite being arrived at. It becomes ever stronger until this power is itself perceived at the boundary of the realm of shadows as a spiritual reality. This happens initially in formative thinking, where one does not only reflect something but where the creative formative process is inwardly 'executed' by the fluctuating movement that leads to the arising of the form.

If one continues to cultivate only the aspect of formative thinking, this has a tendency to go astray. One must at the same time work with the other aspect, with the phantoms of sense-perceptions, in order to arrive at their sources. Both with thinking and perceiving, the original sources lie in the realm of the etheric. Only in human consciousness are they at first separated from one another. Once we have achieved an active, formative thinking, this new step must also be taken with pure sense-perceptions.

To clarify this, an example shall be given at this point. One is sitting on a bench in a forest out in the country; one shuts one's eyes and tries to carry out some very intense meditative work. In the course of the meditation one completely forgets that one is sitting on the bench; but at the end of the meditation the surrounding world reappears. And now one can make a discovery with respect to sense-perceptions. If there are a few leaves that are rustling a little and one is sitting normally on the bench, the sound that one hears is quite soft; but if one is emerging out of a deep meditation it sounds like an uproar — though only for a couple of seconds — then all is back to normal. What has taken place here? For a brief moment one has suddenly been living directly in the sense-perception in the complete absence of phantom or mental image. Through such an experience one may judge the extent to which qualities are subdued in all ordinary sense-perceptions.

Another example. As I go to sleep I touch the bedcover, and there is quite a racket all of a sudden. On the threshold between sleeping and waking, when we are somewhat out of our body, the phantom-like element disappears, the ordering of mental images is loosened, and sense-impressions are thereby experienced far more intensely. Children not infrequently experience this, and some are frightened because they do not know what is going on. It is no bad thing if the adults around them do.

Thus there are two aspects. On the one hand, an ascent to an active thinking faculty, to a formative thinking; on the other hand, the ascent from the phantoms of sense-perceptions to their source in the kingdom of the elements. And now both begin to work together, as in a breath. With every step forward that is strengthened through formative thinking, the extent to which the true qualities of the world of sense-perceptions are absorbed is widened — and also the other way round. This uproar of the reality of the world of sense-perceptions, of the elemental world, disappears in the very next moment unless it is absorbed through formative thinking. If the two begin to work together, a new breath begins — though now not in the air but between thinking and sense-perception. Each is strengthened by the other.[2]

In this activity, the individual experiences the etheric world, his own etheric body, though at first only a tiny corner of it. I should like to express this pictorially — though not only pictorially — as follows: the etheric around the head is the first portion which is taken hold of in this way. This little 'corner' has, however, the tendency to disappear at once from one's consciousness unless a further strengthening is achieved. I should like to indicate some ways in which this can be done.

The first is as follows. If one thinks that one is making some progress in this realm of perceiving and thinking and at the same time supposes that one's own personal life can be left unchanged, that is a great illusion. For this little portion is connected not only with the nearest etheric realm of the head but with one's entire etheric body, which is an organism that lives in time and throughout one's biography. If one does not at this point begin to work upon one's life, the consciousness in the etheric 'corner' remains small and weak. One can, therefore, attempt to strengthen it by reviewing one's life, situation by situation, year by year, backwards as far as childhood, and then contemplating it from a higher vantage-point, not getting steamed up in one's personal life but looking down upon it as though it had been experienced by another person, with the same degree of objectivity, distinguishing the essential from the non-essential. In such a way do we, gradually, live into the true formative forces of our biography. Every time that a part of life is assimilated in this way, there is an element of feedback. The little corner of 'thinking and perceiving' begins to grow, becomes bigger and stronger, and — conversely — a light streams from this tiny corner into the life-assimilating process. It immediately becomes apparent that if I do not work upon my life, this corner remains small and is forever disappearing.[3]

A further path of strengthening is taking hold of the 'time-organism'. Having abstract knowledge about the time-organism is not the same as knowing the reality of it. It must be experienced *directly!* So let us begin with what is immediately around us. We may take this situation here, this evening lecture in this moment, and shall imagine hypothetically that it is now seven o'clock in the morning and that we are all sitting here, and I am standing here and speaking. It would be a *completely* different situation, and it would be a completely different lecture, even if I were to speak the same words. It would be a morning mood: waking up right out of sleep, before breakfast — that would be an altogether different reality. Meanwhile we have got through the day, we have had lectures, conversation groups, and we are moving into the evening. Now let us imagine that it was one o'clock at night — again, it would be a quite different lecture, a wholly different situation.

Everything that happens is what it is, not through the content of the moment but through its position in the time-organism. Where am I in the course of day and night? What comes towards me? What lies behind me? We are always within many small, larger and large circles; the small day — night circle, the whole month, the whole year. We might, for example, imagine that it was not March, and the whole situation would again be quite different; we would be at another point in the organism of the yearly cycle. We can think this through quickly and see that it is so, and we may put it on one side and rumble on from moment to moment and do not really feel the reality of the time-organism. *The feeling* must be *cultivated* that we constantly find ourselves in smaller and larger circles of time and that the small, momentary ones only have significance and value through their relationship with the whole.

When one falls out of the time-organism, nervousness arises. Nervousness also arises from other reasons. When the ego simply leaves all soul-forces and everything that surges within them — thoughts, feelings, wishes, instincts and desire — to take their course and does not take hold of them, the astral body becomes feeble and slack. The astral body has a great fullness in itself, but if the ego does not drive it forward and begin to work within it, it becomes slack. What is the consequence? The astral body can no longer inspire the etheric body, and now the etheric body also grows slack. What does slack mean? It means being dependent on outer, purely fortuitous influences from without. The weak etheric body loses its hold on the physical body, the physical body falls somewhat 'out of sync'. Not completely — if it were to fall completely out of line we would die. But if the physical body falls a little out of line, nervousness and various sorts of illness arise. The physical organism begins to have convulsive tendencies and becomes self-dependent. The opposite occurs if the ego works upon its own soul-forces, upon instincts and desires, and makes *something* out of them: becoming more human, more true in thinking, in feeling and willing, in all inclinations, in all ways of behaviour — that is man *in the becoming*. It is not a case of being perfect, one must not become as perfect as the ideal, that would be a completely distorted way of thinking about it and would also be unattainable — what matters is the beginning, bringing about a change of direction within the will, for such a change already has within it the power of man in the becoming. At once the astral body becomes more taut, stronger. It is no more full than before, but everything becomes at once quite different in it when this inspiring power comes from the ego and the 'becoming of man' begins — immediately the astral body is able to inspire the etheric body with greater strength, and the etheric body becomes less subject to allergies and more vigorous and is able to take the physical body in hand, ordering, health-bringing, healing. We have here a basic element of what Rudolf Steiner calls 'hygienic occultism'. Out of the innermost spiritual powers of man in the becoming, healing forces are awoken, initially within one's own being and from thence they ray out into the social organism.

When a power summons forth 'man in the becoming', the

etheric body is strengthened out of the ego, and this power is borne upwards. The little 'corner' begins to become stronger, it broadens out.

Another path of strengthening, and a *very* important one, can be described as follows. Every individual of the present time has initially the following attitude. He imagines himself to be a small, a tiny, speck on the Earth and endowed with a wholly subjective soul-life, while out there is a vast universe with distant stars with which, however, he has absolutely nothing to do. Even if I make some progress in a moral sense, the whole world of the stars — viewed from an astrophysical point of view — has no connection with this. If one has an idea of this kind, one will *remain* small and weak. One has not discovered what really matters: that this 'something' which awakens in the etheric is not only in me. So where is it? It is — at the same time — also on the far horizon, in the periphery. In the physical realm objects stand next to one another. A physical body can to some extent be separated off, even where one merges with another, as through air and warmth and so on. That is not the case with the etheric body. How should the etheric body be thought of in relation to the whole etheric world? In just as strong a connection as that existing between the physical head and the whole of the rest of the organism! The head is somewhat set apart, on its own, but there is the neck, which makes the connection with the rest of the body and without which it would be unable to live. Man's etheric body also has a certain degree of autonomy, but only to the extent that the physical head is autonomous with regard to the physical organism as a whole. What is the corresponding 'remaining organism' for our etheric body? The *entire* etheric world outside of us! Each human etheric body is like a little head, which belongs to the whole organism out in the wider world. There is nothing here in the realm

of the etheric which does not at the same time work as a
peripheral force in the universe. The physical occupies a
point, and has weight. The etheric is always in the widths of
space, inweaving, absorbing.

The starry world is present — unobserved — as one first
awakens in the etheric, where formative thinking and perceiving are enlivened, even though one may as yet know
nothing of it. The *whole* is present unobserved — and now,
again, a path of strengthening emerges. This life in the whole
must be made conscious, it must be cultivated. One needs to
feel equally at home in the starry periphery as in one's own
etheric body. There are some words in a poem by Novalis,
which one at first simply experiences as poetically beautiful
— and then suddenly one sees the profound truth residing in
these words:

> The starry world will flow forth,
> Life's golden draught of wine;
> As we do drink it gladly,
> Like radiant stars we'll shine.[4]

It is not only poetic, it is true. The etheric vault of the
periphery becomes conscious, the small becomes a star and
lives together with the great. It is the reality of awakening in
the etheric.

I have tried to present a few paths whereby strength can be
acquired: working upon one's life, experiencing the time-
organism, the work of the ego on the other members, the
feedback that accrues from this and, finally, the connection
with the great periphery of the world circumference.

At this point I should like to interpose a short consideration of the so-called fourth dimension. It can be a purely
abstract affair, where one simply goes on counting — fourth,

fifth, sixth dimension... and this can be thoroughly analysed through modern mathematics without there being any spiritual value resulting from it. One can look upon it in so abstract a fashion that one says: three dimensions in ordinary space, then one adds, for example, time as a fourth co-ordinate; now there are four with which one may reckon. That is a significance of the fourth dimension that I do not have in mind. I wish to consider the esoteric significance of the fourth dimension, and then something quite different comes about. Where is three-dimensionality, three co-ordinates in space, to be found? *Only* in the earthly-physical realm, where the world of space is experienced. Only here is this externalizing of the three dimensions — and, with it, the crystalline mineral element — possible. But three-dimensionality is not where it all begins, for there is a descent from the highest spiritual world through three stages to a crystallization point in the three-dimensional world of space. How many dimensions — in this sense — are there in the highest spiritual world? None, zero dimensions. Here there is no three-dimensional world of space, archetypes are purely spiritual. How many dimensions are there in the lower spiritual world? One, a linear dimension, though not a line that is bound to the physical three-dimensional world. It is a line which proceeds out of the spiritual world and only expresses itself as a will-orientation. Then — descending further from the world of archetypes — we come to the next stage, to the etheric elemental world. How many dimensions are there here? Two! They are living pictures which are plane-like but not like the planes in the three-dimensional world, such as a wall or a painting; they are not like that. It is activity: as we descend from the archetypes we come to the first and then to the second living activity. Where are these planes? In the whole circumference of the etheric world and weaving in from there, formatively but with a plane gesture, not yet three-dimensional, not yet in a fixed form. Wherever a fixed form arises, it has fallen out of the relationship with the forces of movement and becomes three-dimensional and spatial, physical and mineral.

Thus we arrive at the following line of development:

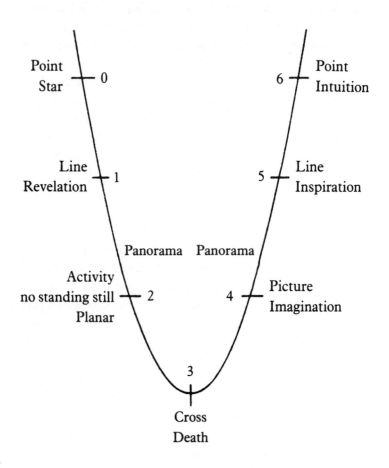

Three-dimensional Space

'Zero' in the highest spiritual world; one could also say 'point', 'star'. Lower spiritual world: 'line', streaming out as a revelation in this realm of the one dimensional. Then comes the etheric world of life, the planar world of activity where nothing stands still. And, finally, the three-dimensional; the cross, death, possible only in the physical world of the senses. It is the descent of a creative activity.

And then begins the ascending line of the evolution of consciousness, and we arrive at the fourth, fifth and sixth dimensions, though not simply as new axes that are added but as an ascent to higher levels where at the appropriate time one dimension of external reality disappears. With the first ascent, one dimension disappears and we arrive at a plane, a picture. Then another disappears — and we come to the line, Inspiration. Again, one falls away — and we are in the point, in Intuition, right in the inner realm of being.

Thus the awakening in the etheric takes place when one's consciousness of the three-dimensional ascends to a higher level, when *one* aspect of external reality disappears and when the plane is not the surface of an object but a living, weaving field of perspective. Where is this field of perspective? There is a very instructive, thought-provoking indication of Rudolf Steiner which sheds some light on this.[5] Where do imaginations arise? Precisely at the point where otherwise memories appear — the realm of Imagination, the imaginative level, is right in those inner regions where one dwells as though at the centre of a plane. What does that mean? It has nothing to do with having visions! A vision comes like a painting from without, one simply beholds it; all possible errors and deceptions can become mixed up with it. The imagination is, in so far as it appears, a product of one's own activity; one experiences oneself in the activity of creating the picture. But at the same time the picture is also in another place. Where? in the infinite distance, in the great periphery. That is the fourth dimension, where one is in the small plane and at the same time in the great circumscribing plane of the periphery, in the starry world.

If one does not pay attention to the starry world, this small inner plane of imagination also disappears, for it can only be grasped if it is simultaneously comprehended as a universal power in the periphery. That is the secret. So what must one do? One must rise up out of one's own little body! That does not mean losing oneself, for in the course of this free deed one can return every time to the three-dimensional and keep a check on one's contact with it, one has complete, conscious security through this contact. If one loses oneself, all sorts of deceptions are possible. One must be able to establish a constant feedback with respect to the point of the cross in the three-dimensional realm. Through this means, one's own freedom is preserved.

Precisely here, however, at the threshold between the second and the fourth dimension (see diagram on page 32), events also take place which make their appearance before birth and immediately after death. Directly before our birth we emerge from the highest spiritual world and come to ourselves shortly before entering the three-dimensional world. Then it is that all the spiritual intentions of the life to come unfold and appear before us as though in a great life's panorama. Immediately after we die the physical body falls away, and now the whole panorama of the past life unfolds — a panorama *before* an earthly life and one *after* it! We are engirdled by the dual majestic life's panorama of our inner-most spiritual intentions — not that we think of all the little details and hence suppose that everything is predetermined before birth, that would be an error. What stand before us after death in pictorial form are spiritual intentions and the spiritual realm of being.[6]

The same is the case every morning as we wake up and every evening as we go to sleep: a panorama of the coming day, a panorama of the day that is past. We are engirdled on a small scale by this circumscribing picturing activity of the realm of being. For what is a picture? If it is a true picture, a being is expressed in the picture; and it will have certain spiritual features that are discernible. It is not an absurd picture which has just been thrown together; it is the countenance of a being which shows what is to come and what has been. It does not disappear during the day but lives in the time-organism directly beneath the surface of the shadows and phantoms and can be made conscious in every moment when this awakening in the etheric begins. Where do I stand now? What is the spiritual direction? A great picture brings this together, and with it I am within this time-organism which moves further on its way.

If one falls completely out of a connection with the spirit, this gives rise to fear. And fear permeates the whole of contemporary humanity because we have fallen out of and have lost this time-organism of the spirit and have, so to speak, cut it up into individual drops in individual bodies. What will happen? Am I hurtling to destruction? Will the whole world be destroyed in the next moment? Fear — rising up out of a deep, black, dark hole. Fear cannot be overcome by merely suppressing it. Courage can be mustered through spiritual activity, for through this one discovers a new relationship with a spiritual reality in which this time-organism may be grasped through one's conscious awareness. One wakes up in it! But even if a human individual achieves something in this direction, he only too easily loses this relationship again. When as a small person walking along the street he starts thinking about the universe, he is completely

filled with what he has learnt through periodicals and the
mass media, a picture of a wholly mechanical, purely material universe where everything that takes place on Earth is
altogether meaningless. If one builds up an exact and
thorough-going mental image of this astrophysical picture of
the world and then imagines that the whole Earth and the
whole of humanity were going to be annihilated in the next
moment, what would that signify for the whole world as
visualized by astrophysics? Nothing! One would presume
that everything would carry on as if nothing, absolutely
nothing, had happened. Contemporary humanity has, therefore, a world-picture through which the whole of its own
existence is annihilated. This gives rise to fear in the sub-
conscious.

Thus this whole astrophysical picture of the world, which
lives like a great massive lump in our consciousness, must be
set in motion, must be raised up into the time-organism,
though not into an astrophysical time which is merely a
co-ordinate axis taken to infinity and is hypothetically shifted
backwards and forwards, always repeating the same thing,
but into the real time-organism. Where does this time-
organism originate? We find a study of this in Rudolf Steiner's *Occult Science*.[7] Here we can familiarize ourselves with
the stages of planetary evolution: Saturn, Sun, Moon, Earth
— evolution unfolds by stages out of the spiritual ground of
being, out of the highest spiritual world, down to the point in
the middle where the three dimensions in the dead crystalline
world become a possibility; then in a great swing on into the
future, where everything that was given, bestowed, assimilated and developed through the stages of descent can be
carried forward in a new, transformed guise in man in the
becoming, in the Earth which is *becoming*. We can ask ourselves: what feeling corresponds to the Saturn stage in the

mood within this whole time-organism, whose seven stages together form a whole? The Saturn mood is Spring, cosmic Spring. What is the mood of Sun evolution, when the seeds that were planted in the first evolutionary stage of Saturn, this world of warmth, spring into life? It is Summer, cosmic Summer. What mood lives in the Moon evolution? Now something begins to fall apart, to split, problems start appearing — the Autumn mood is in the Moon epoch! And now comes our Earth age. That is the cosmic, planetary Winter time; a snow landscape, an ice landscape (from a cosmic point of view), a three-dimensional, dead, crystalline world, cosmic Midwinter! And now imagine that one is gazing out upon the wonderfully beautiful snow landscape and that one did not know that beneath the snow and the bare branches the buds of the coming spring were already formed — then the Winter would be death-bringing, terrible. Winter is wondrously beautiful as a transitional phase, if one also knows that beneath this cold blanket there are already the buds of the coming Spring. I can wait peacefully, enjoying the snowy landscape, until the new Spring comes.

So what is the astrophysical picture of the world? It is a cross-section through the age of Winter, when one has forgotten the ages of Spring, Summer and Autumn which have wholly passed by, believes that there is only ice, snow and Winter and knows nothing of the buds that are in readiness for the coming Spring. A section which at the same time asserts what is false. It is a half-truth, because all the details in the description of the ice landscape are correct. One cannot overcome this lie by saying 'Ice crystals do not exist', for they do — but they must be raised up into the great time-organism, into the awareness of cosmic Spring, cosmic Summer and cosmic Autumn. Then one sees the present picture of death, but at the same time everywhere beneath the surface the buds of the coming Spring. Fear is overcome and one gains an unshakable assurance from the spiritual realities of this great time-organism. This must, however, be *cultivated*. Hence the thorough study of Rudolf Steiner's *Occult Science* is of fundamental importance for the awakening of consciousness in the etheric.

This must then be carried forward and divided up into the cultural epochs. Here again a sickness of the present is manifested: it is devoid of history. That is to say, people know an infinite amount, millions of details about the past, very often correctly portrayed — and yet they are only a half-truth, because they have not been raised up to the level of the great sevenfold steps of the cultural epochs, the Indian, Persian, Egyptian and Graeco-Latin epochs. We are now in the fifth, and a sixth and a seventh will follow. We are on a path where each individual, every moment, has his/her/its full worth and yet only finds an inner significance through the totality, through the whole circle.

And from the great rhythms of time everything comes down to the small rhythms, to one's own life. Even my own life from birth to death is a time-organism, a whole. I am at the present moment in a certain place. Supposing I am 18 years old or 70 years old, what does that mean? That this part of me is given particular emphasis in the physical! The whole of the rest of the life is also there, in the background, above, below, around and about, in the periphery, in the plane which both passes through me and extends into the furthest widths of the horizon. The whole of life is present in every moment, but specific parts of it are particularly emphasized: the eighteenth year of the youth or the seventieth year of the old man. What remains in the background for the youth? Everything that is still to come. This is then present with particular power in the *rest* of the time-organism. What lives especially strongly in the etheric organism of a 70-year-old who has become physically old? The whole period of youth!

There is a wonderful moment in Rudolf Steiner's first Mystery Play[8] where Johannes Thomasius, the painter, goes through inner trials. He experiences the zero-point of shadows and phantoms when he feels himself to be nothing and rises through the questing power of knowledge to this gradual awakening in the etheric. And then he sees two men, whom he knows in the physical realm as the old Professor Capesius and the young Dr Strader. But now the picture broadens for him; he sees the Professor who is old in physical life as a youth! And he sees the young Dr Strader as an old man! It is complementary, because what is emphasized in the physical at the one point calls forth with particular power the opposite aspect in the whole time-organism. The trial of the ego goes through all the phases of this whole of *man in the becoming*.

The time when man in the becoming is strongest in us is, although we do not realize it, when as a small child we are learning to walk, to speak and to think. But man in the becoming works beneath the surface in this etheric sphere of activity throughout the whole of life out of the innermost reality of the divine. Thus with the awakening of consciousness in the etheric we see many layers, many spheres, and they have the property of mutual strengthening. The wonderful thing is that one simultaneously experiences the great and the small; one finds oneself, the element of becoming, in one's own biography, and one finds mankind, human evolution, as I have tried to illustrate by means of the example of *Occult Science*. One finds the truly essential in one's own individuality, the essentially true in man in the becoming; but if that were all, it would be erroneous, for it is only valid if at the same time it lives on a wider scale.

As a fact arising out of the depth of experience it can also be expressed as follows: Christ is found within, in each human individual, but at the same time as the cosmic Christ on a wider scale, in the other person and in the whole of humanity. He cannot be found only in one place. He works in from out of the periphery and at the same time in the depths of the heart.

I have tried to delineate some basic principles regarding the overcoming of the split between inner and outer reality, and I believe it to be clearly evident that here, too, are the wellsprings of the art of education; for, after all, our concern in this respect is with man in the becoming. How can we help children if we do not ourselves make man in the becoming conscious within us? Only through this wellspring can we also be of help to children and young people and encourage them on their way.

THREE

The four qualities of the etheric and the teacher's path of schooling

The first steps on the meditative path of knowledge lead to an inner strengthening of thinking. Whatever the content of a meditation may be, it is a matter of dwelling upon a certain picture in words and thoughts, of being able to move slowly and precisely from one thought to a further thought, so that the whole lies in an inner time-organism in one's consciousness. Thoughts become structures that are wholly permeated with life and enter into movement and, hence, manifest their real nature. This is not the case with ordinary mental images, for these are the reflections of something different; if they are to be clear it must be possible to take firm hold of them. On the meditative path of knowledge, man rises from this foundation of dead mental images to a living, formative thinking. [1]

It is the eternal individuality that gradually awakens to activity in this way. In the brief time-span of such inner activity, everything that proceeds from the physical body — all sense-perceptions — is repulsed. That is, for instance, also the case with perceptions of touch, so that a feeling of hovering appears.

During the course of meditative activity, ordinary mental

images will also constantly seek to manifest themselves. One tries, quite understandably, to make it clear to oneself what one has experienced, one wishes to seize hold of it by turning it over in one's mind. We are in a frontier region, where this inner activity seeks a relationship with ordinary mental images, and we shall learn to conduct ourselves rightly here if we compare the quality of a purely meditative life with the quality of conceptual activity. If we try to compress meditative experience into mental images, we become aware that mental images have something second-hand about them; we see that these 'second-hand' mental images are merely signposts, which point towards something that is truly real. They are not the thing itself. The spiritual fact itself can only be experienced directly.

In what way does one experience the difference between a physical, sense-perceptible fact and a mental image? In the physical realm of the senses one may come up against an object and one knows very clearly: what I have come up against is a reality even if I do not as yet understand it. It is quite another matter if I only have the mental image of, say, a table — the experience of the reality is lacking!

In meditative activity one is affected by spiritual facts, one as it were comes up against them. However, they never come from without. And yet what is a spiritual fact? It is a being or a relationship between beings. There is nothing externalized in the spiritual world. It has the nature of a fact and appears as such in meditative activity. If I form a mental image of it with my ordinary conceptual powers, I cease at once to have the feeling of hovering, of being detached from the physical body. I experience the mental image, which is merely the reflection of something else, as residing in the head, bound to the brain, as it were sticking to the brain — though the word 'sticking' is too weak.   If something is stuck it can be loosened, and the mental image would then to some extent hover over it. But this it cannot do. It is bound up as firmly with the brain as gravity is with matter. One cannot think of the force of gravity without at the same time thinking of matter — and vice versa, if one thinks of matter this is inseparably bound up with gravity. In exactly the same way, ordinary mental images are bound up with the brain, the head.

Now the activity of the eternal individuality enters into the situation, strips away these mental images and directs its whole concentrated attention upon the movement and the life that emerge from its own innermost core.

What do we experience at this first stage of spiritual experiences, as compared to the mental images which stick to the brain? We begin to plumb the depths of the spiritual world, to have a feeling for our own higher being — but it does not appear just like that and only gradually becomes perceptible in the realm of activity within our own etheric body. But our own etheric body can never be thought of without the whole of the cosmic ether in which it is imbedded. After all, it is no mere diluted physical body but is inseparable and unceasingly connected with the cosmic ether, the cosmic sphere of activity of higher beings. Without it, there would be no etheric body.

Now this inner, living activity unfolds, though it does not take hold of the whole of the etheric body at once but initially only a little corner of it (pictorially speaking), the etheric body of the head. In meditative activity one can clearly feel this as a kind of detachment in the region of the head. This inner, living activity in the etheric body arises in and around the brain. At the same time the connection can be made through crossing a kind of threshold to the ordinary mental images sticking to the brain — and then one discovers that the brain and all ordinary mental images are end-products, which have arisen from the sphere of activity of the great cosmic ether. The head, the brain and its mental images are the withered residues of this activity. There would be no convolutions in the brain if these cosmic-etheric influences had not streamed in and moulded the head.

With what mood do we experience this? It has two aspects. On the one hand, we have the deepest veneration and devotion towards the mighty cosmic forces, towards the wisdom that flows together in this wonderful formation of the brain, which alone furnishes the possibility for all our mental images. On the other hand, we are filled with sadness, for we are standing before a withered residue, an end-product, which has within it the seeds of death. We are looking with the deepest devotion into a cosmic past out of which everything has arisen — and at the same time we feel sadness, because we stand at an end, at a final point. What power in the etheric is it which can reach right into this physical forming process, into the end-product? The highest of the four kinds of ether, the life-ether, has this powerful force that works, full of spiritual meaning, into the physical forming process; the warmth-ether, the light-ether and the sound-ether cannot do this. Thus we experience the deepest veneration for these sublime forces, and at the same time a mood of sadness as we regard the dead end-product of the great cosmic forces of the past: melancholy! We have the judgement of the melancholic before us. Hence a person with a melancholic temperament — who lives strongly in the head — tends to look mainly towards the past. He remains attached to what has been. Everything that has taken place leaves so many traces behind it that he comes to a standstill when he considers how it has all come about, what the causes were and so forth. He is past-orientated. Melancholy gives rise to a kind of blue-violet mood in the region of the head. But only a tiny corner of the whole etheric body is active here; the totality of the etheric body has, of course, nothing specifically past-orientated about it, but is permeated by a great, mighty life-force and has past, present and future within it all at once.[2]

And now let us turn our eyes in the opposite direction, push the past aside and we have before us the future, *only* the future — though not a mental image of the future, but a kind of prognosis of the future, for that would again be a wrinkled residue of the past! We must rather in our meditative activity cast our eyes into the real future, and there we find will, will for the deed, courage, warmth! We experience another aspect of the etheric body, the warmth-ether! And so just as the life-ether permeates the entire etheric body — just as it is active in every structural formation down to the toes (for no part of the skeleton is without the activity of the life-ether) even though its own activity unfolds in the region of the head — so is the warmth-ether at work in the whole of the body and only has its *principal* sphere of activity in the limbs. The *structure* of the limbs is dependent upon the head and the life-ether aspect of the etheric body, while their *activity* is dependent upon the warmth-ether. Thus when we look towards the future, everything becomes red, will-permeated, warm — there is courage for the deed; we see the choleric! The archetypal picture of the choleric temperament lies, therefore, predominantly in the limb region of the etheric body.

We now have two poles of the etheric body before us, the life-ether of the head pole and the warmth-ether of the limb-pole, although both also permeate the rest of the body. Whenever there is always activity, the warmth-ether plays a part. In both polar regions the boundaries of the etheric body are annulled: at the head, cosmic formative forces stream in to the brain from the far widths of space, while from the limbs forces are streaming out into the future, forming seeds for future ages.

Now one might say that this description does not correspond with what Rudolf Steiner says in various places. Rudolf Steiner says something like this: In the region of the head the etheric is covered by the physical, whereas in the region of the limbs it extends somewhat beyond it.[3] He draws attention to the fact that one must distinguish between two viewpoints of spiritual-scientific research. The one looks from without into another etheric body, sees it — say — in the colour of peach-blossom; the other experiences the etheric body from within. And in experiencing one's own etheric body one sees these endless streams — of a blue-violet colour — entering the head from above and those red future-aspiring streams extending far beyond the limbs.

And what do we have in between? Between the two poles of the etheric body lies everything that is of the nature of liquid movement, the flowing of the blood, the lymph and all liquids. Here there is no end-product, for nothing ever comes to a finished form, everything flows, streams and meanders throughout the body, forming chemical bonds and separating out again — a flowing interchange. In a pictorial sense the inner colouring is green, comfortingly green, phlegmatic. And from a temporal point of view the phlegmatic lies exactly in the middle, in the present. The *choleric* always has the tendency to disregard the past, he unconsciously blots it out; yesterday is of no interest, what matters is what we are doing now — on into the future! The *melancholic* forgets the future and looks mainly towards the past. The *phlegmatic* meanders and weaves to and fro in the present and is not particularly interested in either the distant past or the far future but is concerned with what is going on at that moment in the watery element of his own body. Here in the middle, in this working of the watery element — where what is of importance is neither the final form nor the intention for the future — lives the sound-ether.

But this middle realm is also permeated by the breaths of man's airy nature. In the case of breaths the pendulum swings much faster than where the movements of liquids are concerned. In man's liquid nature only gentle pendulum movements are discernible, they flow in rhythmical waves without paying any attention to the world and find harmony with one another. The breath, however, streams wholly outwards and then wholly inwards, alternately uniting with the surrounding world and then in the next moment withdrawing into itself. What happens when it goes wholly inwards, when we breathe and hold our breath? Something stiffens up in us, and a kind of self-contained form — approximating to a head-forming process — takes shape. A head-formation does not actually arise, we would not endure that — and we have to breathe out again. And with this out-breathing something streams forth which in its formation represents in embryonic form that out of which something might arise in the world — the *sanguine*!

The sanguine temperament also lives in the present, though not in so absolute a way as the phlegmatic, but more alternating between future and past: hurrying forward with wishes and great plans and then casting a sorrowful glance backwards, laughing a bit and crying a bit, oscillating to and fro. Here is manifested man's relationship to the world, with interest focused in turn more upon the world and more upon himself. In this realm the light-ether is at work.

These four basic qualities in man's etheric body — the life-ether, with its creative moulding process leading to the arising of a form; the sound-ether, which has this tendency to stream together and weave to and fro; the warmth-ether, will directed towards the future; and the light-ether, the revelation of the relationship to the world — are also, of course, present in the great cosmic ether as qualities. However, they only appear in human consciousness if it has been intensified and expanded through a meditatively strengthened thought-process.

———————

If now the teacher seeks to become one who follows the path of self-education so as to be of greater help to children in enabling them better to serve man in the becoming, two large, inwardly related tasks are placed before him.

The one is that he masters these realms — from a cognitive point of view — for his own consciousness, so as to become thoroughly versed in gradually getting to know the world and the human beings growing up in it.

The other, still more important task would be that he cultivates and transforms what he bears within himself of these four forces, so that he makes himself more suited for a truly human encounter with the pupils in his lessons.

If one seeks to gain a knowledge of these four fundamental qualities, one must know that the modern path of knowledge as represented by Anthroposophy always begins at the head pole, in the realm of dead mental images. Here the activity of the individuality, of the true ego, is set in motion and begins to mould thinking in a new and living way. One learns to know the life-ether aspect of the etheric in oneself and in the world.

Dealing with the warmth-ether sphere is an altogether different matter. Here it is not a question of intensifying the inner activity of the will — there is an abundance of this already. The realm of the warmth-ether abounds with impulsive will-initiatives, the choleric life of will proceeds — or, far rather, rushes onwards — without pausing for thought. Here the task is not to make what is dead alive again but to hold back a living, impulsive will-activity and not simply let it run away. And the activity that is awoken in formative thinking must now shine into the otherwise wildly impulsive life of the will; consciousness must be transmitted to the will. But that means *the idea must become an ideal.* What happens if an idea does not become an ideal? Then ideas are rigidified into mental images of the past. Ideas can only be alive if they live in the whole of man's being; then they also become seeds for the future and impart meaning to the realm of the will. Such a fulfilment in the future is possible if the choleric element is redeemed through being at first held back and then — through a ray of enlivened consciousness — irradiated with light.

What happens in the middle realm, that of the phlegmatic and sanguine elements, where the circulation of fluids and the alternation of breaths furnish the foundation for feeling? Here it is not a case of awakening what is dead or bringing consciousness to the will-life, but rather of objectivizing and purifying one's feelings. Feeling-life is for the most part too personal and hence something of a muddle. People tend to live only in themselves. If feelings can be purified and made into an organ of receptivity, 'feelings of a new kind' arise in the realm of the light-ether.

In *Knowledge Of The Higher Worlds* the first introductory chapters are followed by the section entitled 'The Stages of Initiation'. The first stage, 'Preparation', begins with meditations which have to do with the contemplation of what is budding, growing and thriving and on the other hand, with fading, decay and withering. First one observes both these processes with fully awakened senses and then one allows feeling to arise. Thus one is supposed to feel something — though that does not mean instilling feelings into oneself or cajoling them in some way. What is needed is far rather to create a resonance-space where feelings through which the realities of the world may speak can arise. Then 'thoughts and feelings of a *new* character, unknown before, will be noticed rising up in the soul'. At first one may find this surprising, for one has had a wealth of all manner of feelings — though it is obviously not they that are meant. So what are new feelings? They are not mistily opaque but have definite forms. The old feelings are clouded with subjectivism, one has a strong feeling for one's own situation, relates everything to oneself and allows everything else to be coloured by this. Who does not know the situation where one goes for a walk in the woods on a beautiful Spring day and is chiefly aware of oneself, of the wonderful feeling of life that one has when one is going for a walk. These are the *old* feelings: the new feelings form a resonance-organ through which the *world* speaks. In this relationship to the world lives the whole realm of the sanguine element; and deeper tones of association with the world sound forth in the realm of the phlegmatic.

After this initial acquaintance with the qualities of an enlivened thinking, a purified feeling and a will imbued with meaning, we shall now consider the difficult question of the transforming of the four temperaments.

Why should they be transformed at all, can they not remain as they are?

We come on the path of knowledge to a stage where we do not merely slip hurriedly past but are confronted by an existential question: how are these great truths of self and world that I have struggled for related to the rest of my life and to my conduct with regard to my fellow men? Here most people will experience considerable disappointments. Who does not at first have the deep conviction that, if he has achieved real advances in his conscious awareness and has arrived at thoughts that are true and real, the rest of his life can be formed and moulded accordingly? Surely it would be possible to make an immediate beginning? And then one sees: it will not work. One clearly observes the two streams in man which do not at first come together. The one is the stream of knowledge, where a certain degree of enlivening can take place with regard to the dead intellect, and the other is the moral stream of life, which impresses itself upon one's conduct towards other people and the world. That they do not at present for the most part wholly harmonize with one another is something to be very clearly aware of. One can meet a good and loving person with a deeply moral attitude to life — and when one gets to know his thoughts they are foolish and stupid. It is impossible that this profoundly good, loving manner of life could have originated from these foolish thoughts. The converse is even more disturbing: a highly intelligent individual who has cultivated wisdom and considerable knowledge, which he may be able to express in a most wonderful way — and then one sees him quite openly performing immoral deeds. There is a total lack of harmony. An important experience — and the question arises: how does one arrive at a truly valid manner of life where the two streams do not diverge completely? For there is on the one hand something of the present in the striving after knowledge — or in the lack of it — and on the other hand in what one has brought from one's previous earthly life, so that — for example — goodness, love and high morality are simply there as a fact. The task is now to bring the two into harmony, for one should become a whole human being and make the transition

from one's life of knowledge to one's manner of life. If one
tries this, one experiences considerable obstacles through the
temperaments.

At first, all four temperaments with which we are born and
which have unfolded in childhood and youth represent
obstacles. In extreme cases it is not difficult to see the
obstacle, but this is present only in a tiny minority of cases:
the choleric who becomes a real megalomaniac of a tyrant;
the melancholic who develops schizophrenic paranoia and
persecution mania; the sanguine who becomes a wholly irres-
ponsible, hysterical neurotic to the point where he begins to
wander in completely meaningless thoughts, in madness; the
phlegmatic who approaches idiocy. The anti-human and the
obstacle can be observed at one and the same time.

But we are at present considering not the extraordinary
cases but the person who is *somewhat* choleric, phlegmatic,
sanguine or melancholic and who has not worked on his
temperament but simply lets it go its own way. In such a case
we do not have the megalomaniacal tyrant but the difficult
colleague. He is forever treading on our toes, unintentionally
and without even noticing, he cuts across us and shoves us
back a bit and does what he wants — a degree of unconscious,
refined brutality. There is only a very little of the quality of
the tyrant, but it lies in that direction. The melancholic who
is not suffering from persecution mania but is constantly
woebegone, is forever complaining about something, always
finds everything quite dreadful and has some thoughts as to
what is going to happen and is of the opinion that it would be
better if it did not; or the phlegmatic who simply does not
notice anything.

In one of Rudolf Steiner's lectures there is a startling
analysis where he considers all four temperaments and shows
the extent to which they exert a harmful influence upon the

children if they are not thoroughly assimilated by the teacher.[4]

How does the choleric temperament work if it has not been assimilated? Its effect is such that the children become nervous, they have small experiences of shock which become dammed up and come out after perhaps thirty or forty years as an illness of the digestive system. Thus there is a teacher who is giving his choleric temperament the rein — he may not actually box anyone on the ears but he cajoles the child, bellows, 'boxes' the soul and has a shattering effect on the soul-nature of the child. And with this he does not merely harm this one child. There may be girls sitting in the class who are worthy of love, are completely obedient and never give reason for reprimand, and they will eventually be harmed more than the brazen boys who get shouted at; for they have an immense anxiety not that they, but that others could be reproved in this way. The effect invades the entire class, giving rise to digestive illnesses.

Melancholy on the part of the teacher gives rise to heart conditions in later life. The sanguine teacher diminishes joy in life, brings about a lack of vitality. One sees four kinds of illness entering into the children. With a phlegmatic teacher, the children experience a certain vacuum in their alertness and enthusiasm, again and again there is nothing where there ought to be something, where something ought to happen. As adults they become nervous, neurasthenic people. Rudolf Steiner says of this:

'The soul of the child feels a kind of suffocation if the teacher is phlegmatic. And when we search in life for the reason why certain people suffer from nervous troubles, neurasthenia and the like, and go back to their childhood, we again find that the undisciplined temperament of a phlegmatic teacher, who ought to have done many essential things with the child, is at the root of such pathological tendencies. Whole domains of cultural phenomena that are pathological in nature are to be explained in this way. Why is it that nervous troubles and neurasthenia are so terribly prevalent today? You may say that, if these things are true, one must imagine that at the time when people who today are nervous and neurasthenic were being educated, all the teachers were phlegmatic. Well, that is precisely what I am saying.'

And then he begins to modify this and says: Of course there has been a certain amount of variation amongst the teachers, some were melancholic, some sanguine, some choleric and some, indeed, phlegmatic. But over all temperamental dispositions a common surface has, as it were, been painted over, a thin layer of green, of phlegma, and, moreover, a phlegma that is contrary to the spirit. Thus over the four strong colours of blue-violet, yellow, red and green there is an overall film of green, and this green phlegmaticism has given rise to the whole nervousness of our age.

Now we might say: these were the teachers at the beginning of the century, we are not like that. Especially Waldorf teachers will surely not be phlegmatic towards the spirit. But may it not be that a small residue of such a general phlegma is still present? An example: in a certain Waldorf school a chaotic, muddled situation develops shortly before the Summer holidays. A serious observer would be right in saying: now the whole teachers' College should take stock and struggle through to real self-knowledge and then completely change the unsatisfactory circumstances. This would be necessary for the further existence of the school. But what happens? The teachers go into the holidays, the teachers return from the holidays, and the school carries on as if nothing had happened. There is felt to be no need to have a lot of deliberation or to change anything much. Such an outcome is only possible through a certain phlegma, through this ability to gloss everything over with a layer of green!

Another instance: Rudolf Steiner gave the teachers of the first Waldorf school the advice that if one is standing in the classroom and is in a certain sense showered by the insolence of a pupil, one should take this rather as one would a shower of rain where one has gone out without an umbrella. One gets a bit wet, shakes oneself a little — and everything is forgotten. It was clearly necessary to give this advice to the College at that time — but do we need it today? Are we not all too well able to 'shake things off' in this way?

Who has not stood before a class and has been showered by someone or other! Then one sits at home, lowers one's head a bit, then has a little shake, drinks a cup of coffee — and the next morning one is standing punctually in front of the class as if nothing had happened. The sanguine, the melancholic and the choleric do perhaps have to make a little effort to *become* really punctual. The phlegmatic does not need this, he arrives punctually without difficulty, he is in a sense pathologically punctual.

How is it with the matter of addressing the class? The sanguine loves to take part in interesting, also humouristic conversations, but he hops from one subject to another; to remain with one matter only would be tedious to him. The melancholic is silent, it is superfluous to say anything if everything is anyway so miserable. The choleric comes with statements and directions; he speaks about what he wants to do now and what others should do. What is the phlegmatic's capacity with regard to speaking? Neutral instruction, the capacity to be able to give a good, well-disposed presentation with or also without industrious preparation! The faculty of instruction! And here one suddenly gains an insight into the temperamental disposition of a profession! For the teaching profession has this veneer of green, and one must also take heed that the temperament of the profession does not remain unassimilated!

Now every Waldorf teacher will of course try hard not simply to follow his own bent but to transform his temperament, quite particularly if he aspires towards esoteric development. How is it if, say, a phlegmatic wants to pursue an esoteric development?

In the cycle, *The Effects Of Spiritual Development*,[5] Rudolf Steiner speaks of how the phlegmatic will be hard put to it to follow an esoteric path, and then he continues: 'But let us suppose that a phlegmatic person becomes a student of esotericism…'. There would seem to be considerable obstacles in the way. Or is Rudolf Steiner in some way prejudiced agianst phlegmatics? Let us have a look at what he says about the sanguine and his potential capacity to follow an esoteric path. The sanguine becomes a student of esotericism very rapidly and stops with equal speed. He meets with great experiences — and then goes off to do something different. Rudolf Steiner continues: '…so that under certain circumstances the sanguine, as regards his temperament, is the least promising material for esoteric development'. The phlegmatic may perhaps take a little comfort from the fact that he at least has the sanguine beside him. How is it with the choleric — he must surely be suited for esoteric development? Rudolf Steiner: 'The situation is again different in the case of the choleric temperament. It is virtually impossible, or only possible on the rarest occasions, to make the choleric into an esotericist!' Thus as the chances of this happening are virtually nil, cholerics in their impulsive way hardly ever embark upon an esoteric path. Three temperaments are thereby eliminated, and only the melancholic is left. In his quest for deeper and truer knowledge he does indeed arrive at esoteric development. But with him an interesting inversion takes place.

The melancholic who is as yet undeveloped has the tendency to see only the misery of this world: the world is bad and full of wretchedness, and men and women are just the same. After a short time he begins to look in the opposite direction, and the melancholic now sees his own misery and his own unworthiness. Penetrating to the deepest foundations of his soul, he observes what dreadful errors there are in himself; and he does not make any further progress on the esoteric path.

The essential point is, therefore, that none of the four temperaments are initially suited for esoteric development; they are merely obstacles. Man's eternal individuality must first make them suited for it by working on them.

Now let us suppose that the phlegmatic, in spite of his temperament, does after all begin a meditative life and wakes up to the seriousness of life. Thus he practises self-knowledge and looks into the furthest corners of his existence — wholly without any fuss and without getting angry with himself like the melancholic. With a certain objectivity, which is essential for esoteric development, he observes his mistakes. The phlegmatic quality is transformed into the world-objectivity of the sound-ether, where facts appear as they are now in the present. In the cycle referred to, Rudolf Steiner concludes that the phlegmatic, *if* he has undergone a certain soul-development (and it seems to be taken for granted that this is not happening), has the best preconditions for serious anthroposophical development. This is, therefore, a kind of vindication of the phlegmatic, and also, one could say, a vindication of the teacher — though only if the raw material does not remain as it is but is transformed. That is also the case with the other temperaments; man in the becoming must always be encompassed as a whole if one-sidednesses are to be overcome.

If the choleric somewhat reduces the intensity of his pushing and shoving and transmits consciousness into the realm of the will, his power is not lost but is transformed. He becomes the best possible portrayer of the true events of history, because he enters so deeply into the growth processes of the world. And he becomes a person of initiative.

If the sanguine begins to purify his feelings so that the old feelings are quietened, the whole world speaks to him as though in an echo. He will answer with interest for the world and with an inner imaginative faculty, and enter actively into the world.

The melancholic who is able to turn towards the future no longer remains bound up with his own very obvious errors. There is a certain egoism at work if one gets too angry with oneself. One makes the assumption that one had — from the outset — really been good. Now the melancholic looks upon his errors with objectivity and thrusts his way forward — with the thoroughness and the sense of responsibility that are natural to him — to the truth without any compromise.

And the phlegmatic, who would otherwise give rise to nervousness, will — if he transforms his temperament — retain his objectivity, but will also raise the exuberance of life which formerly remained on the lower level in the fluids of his body to the living stream of thinking, into the fulness of life.

After these considerations, we shall hear the closing words of the lectures entitled *Discussions With Teachers*[6] with different ears:

'The teacher should be a person of initiative in everything that he does, great and small. (The transformed choleric, the transformed element of the warmth-ether.)

Secondly, my dear friends, we as teachers must be interested in everything that is going on in the world and in all that concerns mankind. All that is happening in the world and amongst humanity must arouse our interest as teachers. (The transformed sanguine, who lives through the power of his imagination into everything in the world, into all human beings.)

Thirdly, the teacher must be one who in his heart and mind never makes a compromise with what is untrue. The teacher must be one who is true to the very depths of his being. He must never compromise with anything that is untrue, for if he did so we would see how untruthfulness would find its way through many channels into our teaching, especially in the way we present our subjects. (The melancholic who has been transfomed through the esoteric path.)

And the fourth, something which is more easily said than done, the 'golden rule' for the teacher's calling: the teacher should never become stale or grow sour. Clear away the cobwebs and take a breath of fresh air!' (The transformed phlegmatic.)

Thus, man in the becoming, whose influence is now to extend into the etheric body, shines through all four temperaments. And here modesty has a role to play, for what happens if one begins to transform the etheric body? The life-spirit must be developed — that member which will only be fully formed in a distant planetary future — when the entire etheric body has been transformed. Thus we are only in the very initial stages. But what matters is not that one has already achieved something but that one has made a start!

For even the first tiny transformations give a new colouring to the whole of one's life-situation and can then have a healing effect in one's encounters with the pupils.

FOUR

The influence of spiritual beings in the night upon the development of children and adolescents

In our everyday consciousness, from the morning to going to sleep in the evening, we are right on the surface of world-existence. This surface area is an integral part of a deep spiritual reality of which, however, we know nothing in our everyday consciousness. The wonderful thing is that in this thin surface layer we have the possibility of freedom, of establishing our own independent morality, whereas in the depths of spiritual reality — which fills the universe outside us and similarly our own body — there reigns an inexorable spiritual necessity.

Each time we go to sleep, our ego and astral body withdraw from our physical and etheric sense-organs, while at the same time a part of the astral body enters deeply into the hidden spiritual reality of the body. When we awake, this astral body element emerges again and the other part sinks down — and we arrive once more at the level of our ordinary sense-perceptions. [1]

The question now arises: what do we bring from this thin

surface layer into the deep starry realms of the night, and what do we bring with us when we return from these vast starry spaces to the tiny surface of everyday consciousness? If we consider this surface area more closely, we see that it does not only contain the possibility of freedom but also the possibility of doing exactly as one pleases, the possibility of doing nothing of any significance in the course of the day and filling it with empty nothingness.

What happens when one goes to sleep if one has not done anything of significance the whole day but has merely followed one's own inclinations, if one has remained on the surface of things to the point of becoming superficial and has not even noticed that one is living only on the surface?

In such a case we enter into sleep, into the deep expanses of the night, with — in a spiritual sense — empty hands, without fruits, without any yield from the day. And after we have gone through the night and have woken up again, we are not — from a spiritual and moral point of view — where we were before on the previous day but are a little worse off. How is that possible? What happens in the night? When we enter in this way into the depths of the night with empty hands, Ahrimanic elemental beings thrust themselves upon our soul; and the soul does not ward them off, because it has developed an affinity with Ahrimanic beings through the superficiality of the day. A power of attraction has arisen between the soul and the Ahrimanic beings — they find one another, they belong together.

What is the great task that the Ahrimanic beings have to fulfil? They must call forth a sense of alienation from the divine, make the spirit-bereft surface appear for what it is. Such a surface is only created through the withdrawal of the spiritual realm of being, through a denial of the spirit. It is a characteristic of Ahrimanic beings that they are spiritually creative but spiritually creative through denying the spirit. Without this Ahrimanic resistance, world evolution would not make any further progress.

Thus the soul that has become — and remains — superficial is more and more closely united with Ahrimanic beings every time the person concerned goes to sleep and is more strongly influenced by them in the day every time he awakes. With every day, in a downward spiralling cycle of development or vicious circle, it becomes a little more Ahrimanic.

Not that this should be viewed in a merely negative way. Through the intensifying of the Ahrimanic forces, the denseness and firmness of the spirit-denying element that is represented by materialism can take its shape. Materialism is necessary in world evolution, for when it has become sufficiently dense and impenetrable man's innermost spiritual being recoils from it. The individual wakes up, becomes aware of the surface and does not want to remain there. It is the sufficiently saturated and densified resistance through which the soul awakens to a new, purified spirituality. Were it not for recoiling from this resistance, the person concerned might continue in a warm, believing relationship with the spiritual world but would dreamily confuse spirit and matter. Such spirit-dreams of the consciousness may originally have been closer to the divine, but the spirituality weaving within them would not have been pure.

The person who has awoken to the resistance of the surface discovers the new, purified spirituality that lies within him — though it is at first very thin. Only through cultivation and strengthening can it become denser and more substantial, and so grow. How does this happen? Through something being brought into movement at the surface. If a person resolves that he no longer wishes to live on the surface and begins to work on himself, he lifts himself out of an inner,

spiritual power of uprightness above the surface and overcomes the creeping, cringing being that he was before.

This process is closely related to that which the little child
— naturally not out of a pure spirituality but unconsciously
— experiences when it overcomes its crawling state and
stands upright. It is these same forces at a higher level which
are working in the adult when he raises himself up in a
spiritually moral way. In these forces there lives an intense
warmth, an inner energy. This particular warmth associated
with the inner sense of uprightness must be distinguished
from other kinds of warmth, for instance those that work
horizontally. There is an important passage from a lecture
given by Rudolf Steiner on 28 April 1923 in Prague[2] which is
of relevance here:

'The combustion processes (and hence warmth) in man are
completely different from those in animals. When the flame
of an organic being works horizontally, it destroys what
proceeds from the conscience, with the result that what
issues from the moral sphere by way of the conscience is
unable to exert any influence. That in the case of man this
flame is imbued with conscience rests on the fact that, in
man, the flame of the will is perpendicular to the earth. The
child enters into the realm of morality and conscience in the
same way that it acquires a sense of outward physical balance.
In learning to walk the moral aspect of man's nature, together
with his religious sense, streams into the human individual.'

We shall pause for a moment so that we may clearly understand that what is spoken of here is not a rigid, fixed upright
position — the parrot or the penguin has this as well. These
animals are not, however, upright; they are bound in a
particular position and for this reason have a caricature-like

distorted similarity to man. The essential point about a child is that it is able to stand upright — first it crawls and then gradually masters the power of uprightness. Something similar takes place in the case of the adult; first he lies (pictorially speaking) on the surface of the world and merely crawls — and then one day he discovers 'now it is time to stand upright.' A new, higher stage of uprightness has been reached through inner spiritual warmth.

'These are truly sublime powers that enter in when the child makes the transition from crawling to a walking movement. And if we trace these powers back through the darkness of the child's consciousness, they lead us to a still higher association of man with those beings whom we call Primal Beginnings or Archai.'

Who are the Archai or the 'Spirits of Personality'? They passed through their human stage on ancient Saturn, in a condition of warmth, and then continued through the whole of planetary evolution in ever new stages. When humanity had arrived on the Earth, it received the substance, the archetype of the ego, the potential for the ego, from the Spirits of Form (not from the Archai).[3] Whereas the Archai, who are also called Time-Spirits, work in this substance with which they themselves have an affinity as an inspiring, fructifying and nurturing influence both in the little child's acquiring of a moral-religious sense of uprightness and in all entering into an uprightness of a bodily, soul and spiritual kind.

Let us now turn once more to the sphere of our everyday consciousness. If in the course of the day the soul has made some progress towards uprightness, it does not go into sleep with empty hands but with the fruits of this power and this warmth and so comes directly into the proximity of the

Archai. And now the Archai — who are powerless to help if the individual does not bring them anything — are able to strengthen the moral-religious forces of the person concerned, who begins the next day with a new inner thrust, far stronger than he could have managed on his own. Even if it is only a small beginning, the moral-religious capacities of the individual begin to flourish. There is, however, not only the small cycle of day and night but also the greater cycle from one earthly life to another. And many people — children too — have these strengthening Archai forces living in them which originate not from this earthly life but from past lives.

However, we are particularly concerned with the new shoots emerging in this life which are formed in the smaller cycle of day and night in order subsequently to pass over into the greater cycle. When children have such moral-religious legacies from former lives, they can be gratefully received as a kind of miracle. The new growths are not, however, formed by the children on their own but must be nurtured and stimulated by the teacher, by the adults around them.

We are now entering a new and deeper dimension of Rudolf Steiner's indications concerning the practice of education in the basic lectures that he gave when the first Waldorf School was founded. In the first seven-year period, thinking, feeling and willing are still as one, and then these forces begin to grow free from one another. Do we manage to stir the feelings in the lesson in such a way that they unite with what the child is thinking? Gradually the feelings and the will that are initially bound up in the physical become free, they loosen themselves, so that what has been thought can be felt, thus enabling a foundation to be created for the future adult's acting out of insight. If we do not succeed in this, the will remains bound to the physical-etheric organism and is only accessible to animal drives, it remains shallow.

The entire educative process is deeply connected with the relationship with the Archai in the night. They do not interfere but they fructify what we bring by way of little gifts when we go to sleep. The teacher must lead the children in this endeavour. Every time that he overcomes himself even only to a small degree, this power of uprightness is present; and every time that he just lets himself go and 'rolls off' his actions, he approaches the Ahrimanic beings in the night. It is not a question of the number or the size of his deeds but their quality! If the teacher has cultivated this moral-religious 'uprightness' the sublime forces of spiritual warmth, of true egohood, will then be present within him — and he immediately has a stimulating effect on the children.

But this stimulation is not enough on its own. The children must also be guided to find this path themselves. This happens firstly where the substance of the lesson loosens the feeling from all the many drives and longings that are bound up with the body and leads the children to such content as they are able to devote themselves to out of love; and secondly, through every artistic activity. In this way the uprightness of the will can gradually be freed step by step from a wholly body-bound existence and always in co-operation with the Archai.

The little child's learning to walk, and similarly the adult's moral-religious power of uprightness, is the foundation upon which speaking and conversation can unfold in the right way. Again, what is at issue here is not perfect speech but the process which leads from an inability to speak, to learning to speak. Then another, wholly new quality arises alongside uprightness. One must be able to open up and receive what lives in the world, what lives in other people, and enter into a relationship with this. One should also, however, give expression to what lives in the depths of one's soul, for this should not remain locked up but should become manifest. In both directions — from the individual to the world and from the world to the individual — there must be movement, and it must 'get somewhere' in both directions, otherwise no genuine conversation takes place but only chit-chat or monologues. Language creates a union between man's inner and outer world.

Language has at present to a considerable degree fallen prey to the Ahrimanic 'spirits of the surface'. They want to make language shallow, so that it only reflects the surface of things and has merely a signal character, so that it is empty and devoid of quality. What happens when language becomes shallow and empty? Emotion, brutality, crying and shouting pour into this emptiness. Whenever the aspect of quality is removed, the sluice-gates of unpurified emotion open up and language becomes flooded with it.

If we consider this realm (that of speech), we see that there is no security or certainty upon which we can build but that we must constantly be making renewed efforts truly to learn to speak. It is not merely a question of the child's first steps in learning to speak, when one begins to name objects such as table, chair and floor, but of the interaction of the depths of one's human soul with what lives in other people. Even if one has mastered one's mother tongue and has learnt foreign languages, one can examine oneself by asking: can you really speak in a soul-spiritual way, or is your speech merely superficial? Do you tend — perhaps without even noticing — towards conducting monologues and do you suppose that other people understand what you are saying? Is your speech imbued with depth of feeling and idealism, does an interest in the whole vast spiritual universe live in it? And if it is imbued with warmth and enthusiasm, you must examine at once whether this is merely an enthusiasm for what you yourself have to say, an enthusiasm for monologues! At first this always seems to be better than the shallow, boring way of addressing people, but it would be illusory to suppose that it implies a stronger relationship to the world. The teacher does of course have enthusiasm for and interest in the subject that he is speaking about; but his chief task is not that *he* should have enthusiasm but that he should awaken enthusiasm in his pupils — and this, as is well known, is much more difficult. The pupils should enter into the process where they develop warmth in their language and, hence, a living relationship with their surroundings. If they succeed in this, these young souls will as they go to sleep bring fruits into the spiritual world and so acquire a relationship with the Archangels. This warm inwardness of a spirit-filled language is for the Archangels something similar to what air is for us. Just as we need air in order to breathe, so do Archangels need the fruits of the ensouled and enspirited speech of human beings. They experience bitter disappointment if nothing emerges from sleeping souls.

The human souls that enter the spiritual world 'with empty hands' connect themselves once again with Ahrimanic elemental beings, are strengthened by them in their superficiality and enter the next day with an even more shallow and spiritless form of speech. A downward spiralling cycle is set in motion through the influence of Ahrimanic beings, whereas through a speech that is permeated by spirit and warmth of soul — thus establishing a connection with the Archangels — an upward-moving, future-orientated cycle is brought into being.

In the realm of speech, too, there are legacies from former earthly lives which have not been acquired in the present. Nevertheless, we must concern ourselves with the new shoots, for without them the legacies from the past will also be doomed to destruction. We need a new, wholly conscious relationship to the sublime realm of the Archangels. The Archangels look down expectantly towards us and the children — what are souls bringing with them? If even only the smallest efforts can be discerned, the help of spiritual beings will stream down to men and will resound through all their faculties of speech.

The two faculties associated with the powers of uprightness and speech form the foundation for the unfolding of the third power, the faculty of thinking. Already with small children, world-thoughts appear in the simplest form from the moment when they begin to grasp the significance and meaning of things. No longer only through movement and through the word does the child enter into the world but it now seeks a pictorial, inner bond with the meaning of the world. Of course, it would be senseless to speak of materialism in the initial stages of this very first appearance of the world-thoughts. But only all too quickly the wonderful purity of this first comprehension of meaning is 'sicklied o'er' by superficial thinking. The child is wherever possible confronted only with materialistic, spiritless mental images and their combinations, and then the child's initial openness is lost and the living bond with the meaning of the world is thrust into the background. When the child enters school, the teacher of Class One has before him the considerable task of activating the pupil's inner faculty of imagination despite all this superficial information. The children should live in this inner activity, where the soul lives with and enters imaginatively into what the lesson brings. Naturally, the imagination must 'tally' (that is, it must be accurate), so that it entirely accords with the true nature of the matter in question. Thus, in an embryonic way thinking is already being cultivated in all its depth. As a complement to this, the activities of painting, drawing and movement are added. And what happens in the evening, when the children go to sleep? The young souls bring fruits with them into the spiritual world and are led directly to their Angels.

Let us once again consider 3-year-old children, in whom the meaning of the world is lighting up for the first time. Rudolf Steiner says the following about them in the lecture already quoted above:

'It is indeed so beautiful when the child has learnt to think with such directness, in a manner of which most people no longer have any idea at all! The thinking of the child just after it has learned to think is filled with spirituality. It is wonderful to see how — up to the time when they begin to be got at by materialism — sleeping children immediately wing their way to their Angels, how they are united with their Angels during sleep.' (Thus we see that all small children who have only just learned to think fly upon going to sleep to their Angels, and these forces work in a strengthened way into the next day.) 'So we may say that in sleep we seek — though only through idealism, through spiritualizing the realm of thoughts — these words out of which we have evolved in order here to learn the art of thinking as one human being amongst others.'

There was a small reservation here. Children fly to their Angels until the time when they are 'got at by materialism'. And after this they no longer fly to their Angels. When are they got at by materialism? In earlier times, was that perhaps in the years of puberty or possibly at an even later age? Or is it the age between 9 and 10? Is not this time being constantly brought forward, and does not materialism begin to take hold already with the initial stages of learning to think? When televisions have been introduced into children's rooms and children are surrounded with systematic shallowness and superficiality, they are quite definitely being got at by materialism. Rudolf Steiner inserts this observation into his lecture almost as an afterthought. This was at the beginning of the century. Today this afterthought would probably have to be given a large section to itself. It is an assault upon the whole future potential of humanity if such fundamental damage is wrought in these initial stages. We may see that there are tasks for the adult not only at school but in the kindergarten period. He or she must guard the children's first involuntary flashes of awareness of the world around them and try to take them further, so that new shoots may spring forth. What applies to little children also has validity for older ones, for adolescents and for grown-ups; the only difference is that it is manifested in ever-new and ever-changing ways. The creative properties of the day-night cycle should form the background for all thinking activity throughout the whole of life.

We shall now consider imagination somewhat more closely. The important thing here is that the pictures are exact and correspond to reality, and that they stand in relationship to a whole. The specific must proceed from a greater whole, otherwise it has nothing to do with imagination. It is superficial thinking that constantly endeavours to arrive at a particular definition, at a point. One may try to add these points together, so that they can also be put into a computer. Imagination cannot be introduced into a computer, while the separate bits of minute information that are put together through the enormous potential of the computer for making combinations are completely divorced from the activity that leads an individual to his Angel. Instead, Ahrimanic elemental beings are present and work through the night so that the following day the person concerned thinks in an even more superficial and dismembered way than before.

When we strive to develop imagination, we enter into a relationship with sublime beings who bestow moral and religious powers. Here too, what matters is the effort that we make. Sometimes one may have the experience — both in oneself and in one's colleagues at school — of a certain lack of courage with regard to the imagination; but moaning that one does not have enough imagination does not get one anywhere. One is confronted with this or that task in one's teaching and knows very well that pictures ought to be developed out of an exact imagination, but one is unable to accomplish anything. In such a situation one should rest assured that it is the effort that counts. It does not matter so much whether one produces wonderful pictures; what counts above all is the small, intense effort that one makes to stir one's powers of imagination into life. Then something quite astonishing becomes apparent. Even this small attempt that has been made with such difficulty has an effect, it enters into sleep and is strengthened in this realm by one's Angel. The following day this fortified endeavour stimulates the children and awakens in them what is of real importance.

A teacher who has a gift for spontaneity and is richly endowed with imagination by nature will naturally be far more interesting to the children at first than another teacher whose manner of teaching is dry and shallow. But if a teacher with such gifts does not devote himself to the path, his geniality will soon run out of steam. It is precisely this constant endeavour to grow a little beyond oneself that fires the children with enthusiasm. Thus it does not matter so much if one is, to begin with, very weak in this particular area. One needs to recognize what has to be done, make as much effort as possible, and then this faculty will grow and become stronger and stronger. Imaginative activity is quite especially suitable for forming a bridge connecting one with spiritual beings. If one remains on the surface, there is the danger that imagination becomes merely the expression of unbridled fantasy. Imagination also has a need for an apparently remote sphere such as mathematics. A great mathematician always has strong powers of imagination, for he has to discern a great number of, or if possible all, possibilities, and only out of this totality of all possibilities is he able — after much deliberation — to find what he wants. Without imagination he can at best become a master-calculator who adds things together. If even in mathematics the particular can only be arrived at from the whole, how much more must this be the case with all other spheres of thinking! The working of the whole cannot be allowed to get lost in concrete particulars.

There is another, quite different realm where the particular can only be understood by reference to the whole, and that is the great sphere of the workings of destiny and, with it, the possibility of freedom, the possibility of acting out of insight or arbitrarily.

What happens in the relationships of destiny? What part does a person's Angel play in them? The Angel does not create karma — that is effected by far higher spiritual beings. But the individual Angelic being who is near to us lives in our karmic substance, leads and accompanies us; and in the consciousness of the Angel the whole is always present. The Angel knows how the particular event that is imminent in any situation is to come about, he directs and indicates the next steps that we should take on our path of destiny. Thus thinking and imagination are not merely concerned with the working of the smaller and greater cycles but also have to do with the whole working of a person's destiny and with all activity that proceeds from moral imagination.

In the lecture, *The Work Of The Angels In Man's Astral Body*,[4] Rudolf Steiner gives a powerful impression of how our Angel seeks to paint or sketch mighty pictures of ideals in our astral body. However, in the twentieth century he is only able to do this if the individual concerned 'paints with him'. Without this nothing happens. The individual must as he goes to sleep bring something from the day that represents a beginning of such a 'painting together', for then the Angel can strengthen these little shoots and unfold and give substance to the pictures of ideals in the astral body. If he is prevented through the person's failure to do this on this particular day, his activity is transferred to another realm and dreadful caricatures arise as a result. This is not the place to go into further detail. But if one reads on in the lecture, one comes across at the very end, in the last section, a most astonishing statement which one can easily overlook and whose significance one may at first fail to grasp. An exercise, an imagination exercise — and also one of the many karma exercises — is described: one is enjoined to consider inwardly what might have happened in the course of the day but didn't actually happen.

It is possible that we look back over the day in such a way that we see before our mind's eye what did indeed occur, what we have done. The purpose of this exercise is to penetrate to what is essential. But now we are asked to unfold our imagination and consider what did not happen. We might at first find this rather odd — after all, it didn't happen so why should I paint myself a picture of it? We might perhaps forget about the exercise forthwith — until we discover what is important about it. What happens if we really practise this exercise? First, we see the course of events that actually took place, and then we think of a number of concrete images of events which might have happened and how everything would have turned out differently. This is a negative picture of life, negative not in a derogatory sense but in the sense of a contrast, an inverse picture, one that has the same relationship to the first picture, that concave has to convex. What happens through this? We perceive a great richness of possibilities which could have been, and out of this whole there is the one possibility which did indeed take place. If we do this, we arrive at a completely different attitude to our destiny; it is not a mere series of points or straight lines, first this happens and then that, an immutable necessity which simply takes its course; no, we live in a whole as though beneath a great vault, and out of it comes the particular course that events actually took. Rudolf Steiner describes this process in the lecture referred to as follows:

'In the ordinary course of events this does not happen, because as a rule we do not ask ourselves: what was it that was *prevented* from happening by this or that occurrence? We do not usually trouble about the things that have been prevented but which, if they had happened, would have fundamentally changed our life. Behind these things which in some way or other have been kept out of our lives there is very, very much that educates us into becoming vigilant human beings. What manner of things might have happened to me today? If we ask ourselves this question every evening and then think of particular occurrences which could have had this or that result, observations will couple themselves with such questions and introduce the element of vigilance into the exercise of self-discipline. This is something that can be a beginning, and of itself leads on and on, until finally we do not explore only into what it meant in our life when, for example, we wanted to go out, say, at half-past ten one morning and at the last moment somebody turned up and stopped us... we are annoyed at being stopped, but we do not enquire what might have happened if we had actually gone out as we had planned. What is it that has been changed? I have already spoken here in greater detail about such matters. From observation of the negative in our life — which can, however, bear witness to the wisdom guiding it — to observation of the Angel weaving and working in our astral body there is a direct path, a direct and unerring path that can be trodden.'

Thus firstly there are the great pictures of the ideals that the Angel seeks to impart to man's astral body — a process which requires the active co-operation of the human individual. But now the question arises as to how a person gains access to his Angel. The sure and true path lies through this exercise: developing an imaginative understanding of the course of one's destiny, so that the whole — which also lives in one's thinking, for every thought-crystallization is born out of this whole — is now comprehended in this inner dimension. It is a case of gradually arriving at the possibility of freedom, where one acts out of insight and does not merely leave things to chance but participates in the weaving of destiny, working together with one's Angel and immersed in his wisdom-filled guidance. And in the same way one will be able to work together with the Archai through the moral-religious power of uprightness and with the Archangeloi through learning to speak in the deeper sense indicated.

This also applies to the teacher. Of course, the children are not able to carry out such exercises themselves. But they need the adult who is on the path towards establishing a bond with his or her Angel and who becomes more and more interesting for them as a result.

The teacher who is strengthened through the night has a

stimulating influence, and what he does in the course of his teaching begins to take on a different hue. He learns to perceive with ever greater clarity what streams forth out of the night. Who has not experienced that when something has been achieved in a small way in a lesson the children come the next day — the night lay in between — into the lesson as though out of a refreshing bath, and one can feel in touch with the starry realms of the night! And on the other hand, who has not suffered the dreadful agony of knowing that the lesson has not succeeded, that it did not get beyond the superficial and that everything becambe emotional, the children romped and the teacher bellowed. The downward spiral associated with the Ahrimanic beings has begun. We have entered a battlefield where we have the possibility of awakening in our superficial world to a purer spiritual element, one which can gradually become denser and more saturated through working together with the Angels, Archangels and Archai.

If we now turn to the first lecture of *Study Of Man*,[5] we read that the task of the teacher is to help the children to learn to sleep properly. Now children in general sleep far better than adults do, and apart from the exceptional cases when — because they are disturbed in their sleep or are ill — they do not sleep, they usually sleep extremely well. So it cannot be this that is meant. The point is rather that children must learn to acquire a right relationship with the Angels, Archangels and Archai, in that with the help of the teacher they do not go into the night empty-handed but are able in their thinking, feeling and willing to carry into the night fruits of love and devotion. This is a threefold way of learning to sleep properly, and it can enable a new invigorating stream to flow out of the night into the next day.

If one has clearly grasped this connection with the Third

Hierarchy, a new light will also be shed upon the great deed of inauguration that Rudolf Steiner accomplished in founding the first Waldorf School. The spiritual deed of founding the school — which was the wellspring of the whole Waldorf School movement — must necessarily have been wrought in collaboration with the Angels, Archangels and the Primal Beginnings.

This mighty perspective has been placed before us precisely in the century when Ahrimanic beings of varying degrees of magnitude are making every effort finally to break off man's connection with the true divine-spiritual world. In the lecture already referred to, *The Work Of The Angels In Man's Astral Body*, there is an important sentence. Rudolf Steiner says that this working together with the Angels must have been achieved before the beginning of the third millennium. 'As we know, the third millennium begins with the year 2000.' Thus, he does not leave it in the air but makes it quite clear that by the year 2000 what can bring us into a real union with the spiritual world must have taken place. We therefore have only very little time before the great decisive battle, before this crucial moment in world history!

REFERENCES

ONE

1. Jean Piaget, *Six Études de Psychologie*, Paris 1964 (English translation *Six Psychological Studies*, Random House, NY, 1968); H. Ginsburg and S. Opper, *Piaget's Theory of Intellectual Development*.

2. See Rudolf Steiner's lecture of 10 March 1910, reproduced as 'Man: Positive and Negative' in *Paths of Experience*, Rudolf Steiner Publishing Co., London, 1934.

3. A description of this exercise in a wider connection may be found in Rudolf Steiner's lecture 'Das Anschauungserlebnis der Denk – und Sprachtätigkeit' of 20 April 1923, reproduced in *Was wollte das Goetheanum und was soll die Anthroposophie?* (GA 84).

4. Regarding this exercise see the chapter entitled 'Inner Tranquillity' in *Knowledge of the Higher Worlds: How is it Achieved?* Rudolf Steiner Press, London, 1976, and Rudolf Steiner's lecture of 12 December 1918, reproduced as *Social and Anti-Social Forces in the Human Being*, Mercury Press, Spring Valley, NY, 1982.

TWO

1. Rudolf Steiner, *Anthroposophical Leading Thoughts* (No. 1), Rudolf Steiner Press, London, 1973.

2. See Rudolf Steiner's lectures of 30 November 1919, reproduced as *The Mission of the Archangel Michael*, Anthroposophic Press, NY, 1980, and of 3 October 1920, reproduced as *The Boundaries of Natural Science*, Anthroposophic Press, NY, 1983.

3. See Rudolf Steiner's lecture of 15 April 1923 reproduced in *Was wollte das Goetheanum und was soll die Anthroposophie?* (GA 84).

4. 'Die Sternwelt wird zerfließen
    Zum goldnen Lebenswein
    Wir werden ihn genießen
    und lichte Sterne sein'   (From *Hymns to the Night*, V)

5. See *Die Bedeutung der Anthroposophie im Geistesleben der Gegenwart* (GA 82), six lectures and a seminar given 7 – 12 April 1922 at The Hague. (Two of these appear in English translation in *The Golden Blade 1961*, Rudolf Steiner Press, London.)

6. Rudolf Steiner, *Occult Science - An Outline*, Rudolf Steiner Press, London, 1969.

7. ibid.

8. See 'The Portal of Initiation' in Rudolf Steiner, *Four Mystery Plays*, Rudolf Steiner Press, London, 1982.

THREE

1. As a fundamental contribution to this theme, see Jörgen Smit's essay, 'Der meditative Erkenntnisweg der Anthroposophie' originally included in *Freiheit erüben* (Stuttgart, 1988) and reproduced as *How to Transform Thinking, Feeling and Willing*, Hawthorn Press, Stroud, 1989.

2. For this and for what follows see Rudolf Steiner, *The Effects of Spiritual Development*, Rudolf Steiner Press, London, 1978. (Ten lectures given 20 – 29 March 1913 and previously translated as *The Effects of Occult Development upon the Sheaths of Man*, Anthroposophical Publishing Co., London, 1945.)

3. See lecture 4 of *The Effects of Spiritual Development* (ref 2 above).

4. Lecture of 8 April 1924, reproduced as lecture 1 in *Essentials of Education*, Rudolf Steiner Press, London, 1968. (English translation revised by Jesse Darrell.)

5. See lecture 3 of *The Effects of Spiritual Development* (ref 2 above).

6. Rudolf Steiner, *Discussions with Teachers*, Rudolf Steiner Press, London, 1967. (Closing words to Discussion XV, 6 September 1919.) Translation based on that by Helen Fox.

FOUR

1. For this and for what follows see Rudolf Steiner, *Die menschliche Seele in ihrem Zusammenhang mit göttlich-geistigen Individualitäten* (11 lectures given between April and July 1923). Four have been reproduced in English translation – two in *The Waking of the Human Soul and the Forming of Destiny*, Steiner Book Center, Vancouver, 1970; one in *The Festivals and their Meanings*, Rudolf Steiner Press, London, 1981; one in *Man's Being, His Destiny and World Evolution*, Anthroposophic Press, NY, 1966.

2. See *The Waking of the Human Soul and the Forming of Destiny* (ref 1 above).

3. See the chapter entitled 'The Nature of Man' in *Occult Science - An Outline*, Rudolf Steiner Press, London, 1969.

4. Rudolf Steiner, *The Work of the Angels in Man's Astral Body*, Rudolf Steiner Press, London, 1972 (a lecture given on 9 October 1918 in Zurich). Translation by Dorothy Osmond assisted by Owen Barfield.

5. Rudolf Steiner, *Study of Man*, Rudolf Steiner Press, London, 1966. These were the fourteen fundamental pedagogical lectures given to the teachers of the first Waldorf School in 1919.

ESSAYS ON EDUCATION
Francis Edmunds

The name of Francis Edmunds will always be a part of the Rudolf Steiner Education movement. He has travelled widely and his talks and writings, emphasising the responsibility of adults and educators towards children, have inspired and educated a worldwide audience. This collection of essays covers many different subjects and will be an obligatory reference work for all teachers. The essays are also invaluable to all concerned with the spiritual basis of an individual's development from childhood onwards.

217 × 138mm; 136pp; paperback.
ISBN 1 869 890 31 0

THE ORIGIN AND DEVELOPMENT OF LANGUAGE
Roy Wilkinson

Many years of working as a Waldorf teacher enable the author to offer a wide-ranging survey of the origin of language. He traces language from its spiritual roots to the almost soulless polyglot that we call language today. He enthusiastically uncovers the many layers contained in the English language, and discusses how we can rediscover a true way of knowing how, and what, we speak.

217 × 138mm; 96pp; paperback.
ISBN 1 869 890 35 3

CREATIVE FORM DRAWING
WORKBOOKS 1, 2 & 3
Rudolf Kutzli

Translated by Roswitha Spence

Workbook 3 is the latest in this successful series. Readers are encouraged to explore in detail the ways in which forms are created. The exercises give fascinating insights into the relationship between form and content. *"...a most unusual offering in which form and content are indissolubly wedded, and in which the crossing point of the two consists of our own activity."*

297 × 210mm; 152pp; fully illustrated; sewn limp bound.

Workbook 1   ISBN 0 950 706 28 0
Workbook 2   ISBN 0 869 890 14 0
Workbook 3   ISBN 1 869 890 32 9

THE LISTENING EAR
Audrey E McAllen

The development of speech as a creative influence in education.

This book gives teachers an understanding of speech training through specially selected exercises. These aim to help develop clear speaking in the classroom, and to assist those concerned with the creative powers of speech as a teaching tool. The author looks at the links between speech and child development, the speech organs, the effects of artificially produced sound on speech development, rhythm, metre and the sound groups.

210 × 135mm; 162pp; 36 illustrations; sewn limp bound.
ISBN 1 860 890 18 3

SLEEP
Audrey E McAllen

An unobserved element in education.

Sleep presents research on the experiences of the human soul during sleep, as a vital but often unobserved element in child development. The use of moral colour exercises are described in relation to therapeutic work with children.

210 × 150mm; 72pp; illustrated; paperback.
ISBN 1 869 890 03 5

DRAWING & PAINTING
IN RUDOLF STEINER SCHOOLS
Magrit Jünemann and Fritz Weitmann

This comprehensive account of painting and drawing in the Steiner curriculum combines detailed practical advice with clearly defined philosophy on aesthetic education. The book takes readers carefully through each stage of Steiner art teaching, suggesting appropriate exercises and explaining the reasons for the different developments in the curriculum at appropriate stages of pupils' development. This book is not only a vital reference source for all who are involved in teaching in Waldorf schools, but an inspiration to all who are concerned with children's creative development and fulfilment.

170 × 240mm; 256pp approx; hardback.
ISBN 1 869 890 41 8

HOW TO TRANSFORM THINKING FEELING AND WILLING
Jörgen Smit
Translated by Simon Blaxland de Lange

This book aims to enable readers to follow a meditative path leading to deepening insight and awareness of themselves and the world around them. Practical exercises for illuminating and strengthening thinking are described, for developing inspiration and intuition and also for exploring the qualities of composure, reverence, open-mindedness and wonder.

214 × 134mm; 56pp; paperback.

ISBN 1 869 890 17 5

SOCIAL TRANSFORMATION
Jörgen Smit
Translated by Simon Blaxland de Lange

Throughout history revolutions have challenged people to transform society on the basis of freedom, equality and fraternity. Attempts are still being made to find a path midway between communism and liberal capitalism. Jörgen Smit argues that individuals can and must take responsibility for developing real freedom in everyday life. He addresses the way rhetoric about equality can be transformed to reality. He looks at ways of liberating work from wage slavery and at the real, rather than the perceived, boundaries of the state, the economy and voluntary activities.

217 × 138mm; 128pp; sewn limp bound.

ISBN 1 869 890 43 4

For further information or a book catalogue, please contact:
Hawthorn Press, Hawthorn House, 1 Lansdown Lane,
Stroud, Gloucestershire GL5 1BJ
Tel: (01453) 757040 Fax: (01453) 751138
E-mail: info@hawthornpress.com
Website: www.hawthornpress.com

If you have difficulties ordering Hawthorn Press books
from a bookshop, you can order direct from:
Scottish Book Source, 137 Dundee Street,
Edinburgh EH11 1BG
Tel: (0131) 229 6800 Fax: (0131) 229 9070
E-mail: scotbook@globalnet.co.uk